...uary, 1856.

E   DAMNABLE'S HOTEL

*Commander T. S. Phelps, U.S.N.,
...er 1979 by Becky Decker)*

 ...ngton Territory, January, 1856.

PIONEER DAYS ON PUGET SOUND

ARTHUR ARMSTRONG DENNY
Born 20 June 1822 — died 9 January 1899

PIONEER DAYS ON
PUGET SOUND

ARTHUR ARMSTRONG DENNY

YE GALLEON PRESS
FAIRFIELD, WASHINGTON
1979

Library of Congress Cataloging in Publication Data

Denny, Arthur Armstrong, 1822-1899.
    Pioneer Days on Puget Sound.

    1. Puget Sound area—History. 2. Denny, Arthur Armstrong, 1822-1899. 3. Pioneers—Washington (State)—Puget Sound area. 4. Puget Sound area—Biography. I. Title.

F897.P9D4   1979   979.7'77   79-23378
ISBN 0-87770-226-8

Mary Boren Denny 1822-1910

Denny Hall, University of Washington, with inset photos of Arthur and Mary Denny.

TABLE *of* CONTENTS

HON. ARTHUR A. DENNY,
A PIONEER OF 1851.

MRS. A.A. DENNY.

LOG CABIN OF A.A. DENNY,
AL-KI POINT, W.T.
(ERECTED NOVEMBER 1851.)

DAVID T. DENNY.

MRS. D.T. DENNY,
SEATTLE, W.T.

NOTES

It is now (1978) 127 years since the Denny Party came to Puget Sound, and 90 years since Arthur A. Denny wrote *Pioneer Days on Puget Sound.*

Few Americans have left more to their countrymen than Arthur Armstrong Denny. As a founder of a great state, a great city, and a great university, he contributed richly to each. For each he was a true founder, the man who dreamed, who worked, and who gave totally of himself to their achievement. Each of these three institutions still bears the mark of his vision and his character as well as of his works, his gifts, his plans.

Arthur Denny was modest with respect to his achievements and enjoined his contemporaries as well as posterity against excesses in celebrating pioneer achievements, particularly his. Yet, at the time of his passing, the Seattle Chamber of Commerce heralded him as the "Founder and Father of Seattle," and the President of the University of Washington compared him with Jefferson for his founding of the University of Washington. In the manner of appearance of the Denny name on streets and buildings in Seattle, Arthur Denny's self-effacement is reflected. Denny Way, James Street, and Marion Street are named after brothers; the two Denny parks are named after a brother and a son; John Street is named after his father and his nephew, and Lenora Street after his daughter. When he became a full partner in Seattle's principal banking institution, he refused an offer to have his name included in the title of the company. Yet, as Clarence Bagley has noted, it was Denny's towering reputation for integrity along with that of Dexter Horton which gave the bank and Seattle its start as a regional banking center throughout the Puget Sound area—a fact significantly contributory to Seattle's emergence as the metropolis of the Northwest. The first building on the present University of Washington campus bears his name, and it is characteristic that it was not so named until after his death and then, as far as imperfect records and memory indicate, named after both Arthur and Mary Denny, although a modern Board of Regents inadvertently omitted Mary Denny's name from an official plaque in the building.

He saw his immense achievements as a public man in frontier America as simply an effort to "meet the obligations to my family and discharge my duty as a citizen to my country and the community in which I have lived." His memoirs were written with reluctance and only to set the record straight. Through all of what he wrote on the events in which he participated, he seems to have been mostly concerned that *his* part in events not be exaggerated and that the role of others be fairly and fully stated. Perhaps no single act better typifies his attitude than a document dated January 1, 1880 in which he convened certain then aging pioneers to make a precise 500 word statement on precisely who arrived first at precisely what places on precisely what dates in "that part of Washington territory now embraced principally in King

County." What is not in his own written record is as important as what is. One can find little or no reference to his many acts of philanthropy, acts involved in the founding of major religious, educational, civic, business, and social institutions in the city and the state through rich gifts, usually of property and always of his own energy, leadership and immense prestige.

His own published writings omit entirely all reference to his role in founding the University of Washington. His and Mary Denny's own rich gift to that institution, which is clearly one of the largest private endowments to a public institution of higher education, and his role in the legislature, as Superintendent of Public Lands and as regent, comprise a noble legacy to that great institution. Above all, his early commitment of his community to higher education well before any comparable commitment in any other place was an act of fabulous foresight, rash and almost arrogant.

One finds no reference to his six children, although he lived long enough to see them all to manhood and womanhood and to know all of his sixteen grandchildren. With one exception—a touching account of his wife's tears at Alki Point—there is no portrayal of the high personal drama of those noble moments of great decision in pioneer history. "It is no time," he said, "for romancing or painting fancy sketches when we are nearing the end of our voyage." Perhaps he anticipated the tragic public misunderstanding of the real meaning of pioneering in the West, a misunderstanding typified by cheap and inaccurate television melodramas which have almost completely deprived Americans of the great sense of heritage and the challenge that the heritage places upon them. The rediscovery of the meaning of pioneer America at a time when an urgent need in the country is the rebuilding of a sense of community is relevant to the present tensions of urban areas. In this context, it is worth noting that Arthur Denny was an abolitionist and a tireless advocate of the rights of Indians as well as their revered friend.

The present volume contains Arthur A. Denny's two principal historical writings. They are *Pioneer Days on Puget Sound*, originally written in 1887, first published in 1888 by Clarence Bagley, second published in 1908 by the Alice Harriman Company, and more recently republished by Ye Galleon Press in 1965; and an autobiographical sketch and brief history of the founding of the State of Washington published in Volume One, Number One of *The Washington Historian* in September 1899 following Mr. Denny's death that year.

It would be appropriate and consistent with the whole style of his life that this brief volume be dedicated to Mary Ann Boren Denny to whom in Arthur Denny's words, "I am very largely indebted for any success which I may have achieved in my life."

Brewster Castberg Denny

Seattle 1978

BIOGRAPHICAL DETAIL

THE LIFE OF HON. ARTHUR A. DENNY.

AN AUTOBIOGRAPHY.

In all ages, the pioneers of the world have occupied a prominent place in its history. They were usually men of action more than of words, yet many of them have left a deep and lasting impression, not only upon their own day and generation, but upon succeeding ages. Abraham was not the first man to "go west" and become the father and founder of a great nation. When the people of our own country were looking for a leader, at a great crisis in their history, they did not go to the cultivated population of its Eastern States and cities, but they went west and took Abraham Lincoln, a pioneer of the State of Illinois, who led them triumphantly through the most critical period of their existence, notwithstanding the manifold and extraordinary difficulties by which he was surrounded. In our own State, the name of Arthur A. Denny is everywhere recognized as that of a man who has borne a conspicuous and an honorable part in its early settlement and in the work of laying the foundations of a great and prosperous commonwealth. For more than forty-seven years he faithfully discharged, without fear and without reproach, every duty devolving upon him, whether personal and domestic or public and official in its character. From the time of his arrival at Alki Point, on the 13th day of November, 1851, to the day of his death in Seattle, on the 9th of January, 1899, he was never known to falter in the performance of any trust or obligation he may have assumed, but during all of that time he was known as an upright, sincere and earnest, God-fearing man, whose highest ambition it was to serve his country and his fellow-men to the best of his ability as a useful, progressive, patriotic and law-abiding citizen.

At his death it was realized that "a great man had fallen in Israel." Yet he came to his grave in a full age, "like as a shock of corn cometh in his season." And his loss was deplored by thousands of people who were nevertheless proud of the fact that such a man had lived and died amongst them. His memory is a priceless legacy, not only to his descendants, but to the entire community in which he dwelt, and to the Territory and State of which he was so long an honored citizen. It has been said that "the best commentary upon any work of literature is a faithful life of the author." If this is true, it is also true that the best memorial which can be framed of such a man as Mr. Denny is the publication of a plain and straightforward history of his personal life and character. Fortunately he has left us an autobiography which will, beyond question, be more interesting to our readers than anything which could be written, no matter how impartial it might be, by a surviving friend or acquaintance.

This sketch of his life is written in that direct and unassuming manner which characterized Mr. Denny, and, like the "Personal Memoirs of Gen. Grant," it carries with it the conviction that it was written by a man of strict and sturdy integrity. This autobiography is as follows:

AUTOBIOGRAPHICAL SKETCH OF ARTHUR ARMSTRONG DENNY.

I have been of late so frequently solicited for a sketch of my life that it has become a source of annoyance, more especially as it has never occurred to me, and does not now, that my life's history is of any importance or calculated to be of any special interest to the public at large.

In my life work I have simply endeavored to meet the obligations to my family and discharge my duty as a citizen to my country and the community in which I have lived. It has not occurred to me that I have accomplished anything above the ordinary, and, if so, I should feel humiliated to claim it for myself.

My life has been a busy one and I have not taken time to think of the estimate which those who are to come after me may put upon what I have done, or whether they will consider it at all. Having reached a time when what I can do, or what I may think or say is of but little moment to the active world, the hard and annoying thing to me is the seeming disposition to dissect the subject before death. It is not, therefore, for self-exaltation that I have undertaken to make as brief a sketch as possible, but to relieve myself of the annoyance referred to, and for the satisfaction of my family.

ARTHUR ARMSTRONG DENNY.
SEATTLE, NOVEMBER 25th, 1890.

SOME NOTES

The Dennys are a very ancient family of England, Ireland and Scotland. I trace my branch from Ireland to America in my great grand-parents, David and Margaret Denny, who came to America before the Revolution, and settled in Berks County, Pennsylvania, where my grand-father, Robert Denny, was born in the year 1753. In early life he removed to Frederick County, Virginia, where he, in the year 1778 married Rachel Thomas, and in about 1790 removed to and settled in Mercer County, Kentucky, where my father, John Denny, was born May 4th, 1793. On August 25th, 1814, he was married to Sarah Wilson, my mother, the daughter of Bassel and Ann Wilson. My mother was born in the old town of Bladensburg, near Washington City, February 3rd, 1797. Her mother's name was Scott, but I cannot trace the families of my maternal grand-parents beyond America, but they, doubtless, came to America in very early times.

Both of my grand-parents rendered service in the Revolutionary War, and my grand-father Wilson belonged to Washington's command at Broddock's defeat.

My father was a soldier in the War of 1812, and belonged to Colonel Richard M. Johnson's regiment of Kentucky Volunteers. He was also an Ensign in Captain McAfee's Company. He was with Harrison at the Battle of the Thames, when Proctor was defeated and the noted Tecumseh was killed. He was a member of the Illinois Legislature in 1840-41, with Lincoln, Yates, Baker and others, who afterwards became noted in national affairs. He was a Whig in politics, and a Republican after the formation of that party. For many years he was a Justice of the Peace, and it was his custom to induce litigants, if possible, to settle without a resort to law; I do not think he was ever himself a party in an action at law. He died July 28th, 1875, in his eighty-third year. My mother died on March 25th, 1841, in her forty-fifth year. For her I had the greatest reverence, and as I now look back and contemplate her character, it seems to me that she was as near perfect as it is possible to find any one in this world.

About the year 1816 my parents removed from Kentucky to Washington County, Indiana, and settled near Salem, where I was born, June 20th, 1822. When I was about one year old they removed to Putnam County, six miles east of Greencastle, where they remained until I was in my thirteenth year, when they removed to Knox County, Illinois. The first land entered in Putnam County by my father was March 12th, 1823. My impression is that he went there and made the selection at that time and moved the family some time in the summer or fall of the same year.

Arthur Armstrong Denny

My education began in the log school house so familiar to the early settler in the old West. The teachers were paid by subscription, so much per pupil, and the schools rarely lasted more than half the year, and often but three months. Among the earliest of my recollections is one of my father hewing out a farm in the beech woods of Indiana; and I well remember that the first school I attended was two and a half miles distant from my home. When I became older it was often necessary for me to attend the home duties one-half of the day and then go to school, a mile distant; but by close application I was able to keep up with my class. My opportunities, to some extent, improved as time advanced, but I never got beyond the boarding school and seminary. I spent my vacation with older brothers at carpenter and joiner work, to obtain the means to pay my expenses during the terms time.

On November 23rd, 1843, I was married to Mary Ann Boren, to whom I am very largely indebted for any success which I may have achieved in life. She has been kind and indulgent to all my faults, and in cases of doubt and diffculty in the long voyage we have made together she has always been, without the least disposition to dictate, a safe and prudent adviser.

I was eight years County Surveyor of Knox County, Illinois, and resigned that position to come to the Pacific Coast. On April 10th, 1851, I started with my family across the plains, and reached The Dalles, August 11th, and arrived in Portland, August 23rd. On the 5th of November we sailed for Puget Sound on the Schooner *Exact*, and arrived at our destination on Elliott's Bay, November 13th, 1851.

The place where we landed we called Alki Point, at that time as wild a spot as any on earth. We were landed in the ship's boat when the tide was well out; and while the men of the party were all actively engaged in removing our goods to a point above high tide, the women and children had crawled into the brush, made a fire and spread a cloth to shelter them from the rain. When the goods were secured I went to look after the women, and found on my approach that their faces were concealed. On a closer inspection I discovered that they were in tears, having already discovered the gravity of the situation; but I did not for some time discover that I had gone a step too far. In fact, it was not until I became aware that my wife and helpless children were exposed to the murderous attacks of hostile savages, that it dawned upon me that I had made a desperate venture. My motto in life was to never go backward, and in fact if I had wished to retrace my steps it was about as nearly impossible to do so if I had taken the bridge up behind me. I had brought my family from a good home surrounded by comforts and luxuries, and landed them in a wilderness, and I do not think that it was at all strange that a woman who had, without complaint, endured all the dangers and hardships of a trip across the great plains should be found shedding tears when contemplating the hard prospect then so plainly in view. Now, in looking back to the experiences of those times, it seems to me that it is not boasting to say that it required quite an amount of energy and some little courage to contend with and overcome the difficulties and dangers we had to meet. For myself, I was for the first several weeks after our landing, so thoroughly occupied in building a cabin to shelter my family for the winter that I had not much time to think of the future. About the time we got our houses completed our little settlement was fortunately visited by Captain Daniel S. Howard, of the Brig *Leoness*, seeking a cargo of piles which we contracted to furnish. This gave us profitable employment, and although the labor was severe, as we did it mostly without a team, we were cheered on with the thought that we were providing food for our families. A circumstance occurred just at the close of our labor which for a few hours caused us the greatest anxiety and even consternation, but resulted in considerable amusement afterwards. We finished the cargo late in the afternoon, and it was agreed between us and the Captain that he would settle with us the next day. The vessel was anchored near the Point, and that night there was a stiff gale from the south, which caused the anchor to drag, and carried the brig before it until the anchor caught in mud at Smith's Cove. The Indians soon discovered it and came and reported that the ship had "clatiwad" (left), which caused in our little settlement great astonishment and concern. We were forced to the conclusion that the Captain had absconded to avoid paying us for our hard work and the time we had put in on the cargo was not counted by eight-hour days, but from daylight until darkness. The ship's unexpected departure added a sleepless night to our arduous toil. In the morning, when it grew light enough to see, to our great joy, we discovered the brig getting under way and she soon returned. The Captain came on shore and gave a most satisfactory explanation, and he was ever afterwards, to the day of his death, the especial favorite of every one of our little community.

In February, 1852, in company with William N. Bell and C. D. Boren, I made soundings of Elliott's Bay along the eastern shore and towards the foot of the tide flats to determine the character of the harbor, using for that purpose a clothes line and a bunch of horse shoes. After the survey of the harbor we next examined the land and timber around the Bay, and after three days careful investigation we located claims with a view of lumbering, and, ultimately, of laying off a town.

I came to the Coast impressed with the belief that a railroad would be built across the continent to some point on the northern coast within the next fifteen or twenty years, and located on the Sound with that expectation. I imagined that Oregon would receive large annual accessions to its population, but in this I was mistaken, mainly by the opening of Kansas and Nebraska to settlement. The bitter contest which arose there over the slavery question had the effect to attract and absorb the moving population to such an extent that very few, for several years, found their way through those territories; and a large proportion of those who did pass through were gold seekers bound for California.

Then came our Indian war, which well nigh depopulated Washington Territory. This was followed by the great rebellion, all of which retarded the growth of the Territory, and for a long time prevented the construction of the railroad upon which I had based large hopes. In the spring of 1852, when we were ready to move upon our claims, we had the experience of the fall before over again in building our cabins to live in. After the houses were built we commenced getting our piles and hewn timber mostly for the San Francisco market; but occasionally a cargo for the Sandwich Islands. Vessels in the lumber trade all carried a stock of general merchandise, and from them we obtained our supplies.

The Captain sold from the vessel while taking in cargo, and on leaving turned over the remainder to me to sell on commission. On one occasion my commission business involved me in serious difficulty. The Captain of one of the vessels with whom I usually delt, carried a stock of liquors, but he knew that I did not deal in spirits, and disposed of that part of the cargo himself or kept it on board. On one occasion, as he was ready for the voyage from San Francisco with his usual stock something prevented his making the voyage himself; he put a young friend of his just out from Maine in command and gave him general directions, but when they came to the whisky, the young Captain said, "What am I to do with that? I will not sell it." "Well," he replied, "take it up to my agent, Mr. Denny, and if he will not dispose of it, turn it over to a friend of mine at Alki Point, who is in the trade." The vessel arrived and the new Captain came on shore with a letter explaining the situation. I told him, "All right, Captain, take it to Alki; I have no use for it." In due time the cargo was completed and the Captain came on shore and informed me that the man at Alki had on hand a full stock of his own and would not take the stuff; and he would throw it overboard if I did not take it out of his way. My obligation to the owner would in no way justify me in permitting so rash an act, and I told the Captain to send it on shore with the goods he was to leave, and have his men roll it up to the house, and I would take care of it until the owner came. I was cramped for room, but I found places to store it under beds and in safe corners about my cabin. It was a hard kind of goods to hold on to in those days, but there was never a drop of it escaped until the owner came and removed it to Steilacoom.

I continued in the commission business until the fall of 1854, when I entered in copartnership with Dexter Horton and David Phillips, in a general merchandise business, under the firm name of A. A. Denny & Co. Our capital was very limited; it would hardly purchase a truck load of goods now, but we did for a time, in a small, one-story, frame building on the corner of Commercial and Washington Streets, afterward occupied by the bank of Dexter Horton & Co., the leading business of the town.

When the Indian war came on in 1855, the firm dissolved and I went into the volunteer service for six months.

I served as County Commissioner of Thurston County, Oregon, when that County covered all of the territory north of Lewis County, and when Pierce, King, Island and Jefferson Counties were formed by the Oregon Legislature I was appointed a Commissioner of King County. In 1853 I was appointed Postmaster and received the first United States mail in Seattle. August 27th, 1853. On the organization of Washington Territory I was elected to the House, and continued a member of either House of Representatives or of the Council for nine consecutive sessions, and was Speaker of the House the third session. I was Register of the United States Land Office at Olympia from 1861 to 1865, when I was elected Territorial Delegate of the Thirty-ninth Congress.

On the 16th of June, 1870, my old friends and business partners, David Phillips and Dexter Horton founded the Bank of Phillips, Horton & Co., and at the death of Mr. Phillips, which occurred on March 6th, 1872, Mr. Horton, although alone in business, adopted the firm name of Dexter Horton & Co. I entered the bank at this time as executor of the Phillips estate, and after closing the affairs of the estate, and took a half interest in the bank under the existing firm name, which Mr. Horton offered to change at the time, but, being fully satisfied with the name, I declined to allow the change.

I have been identified with the fortunes and interests of Seattle from the day of its founding, and during the active period of my life it has been my earnest endeavor to promote and protect those interests to the best of my ability.

My work is practically over. If it has been done in a way to entitle me to any credit, I do not feel that it becomes me to claim it. Should the reverse be true, then I trust that the mantle of charity may protect me from the too harsh judgment and criticism of those now on the active list; and that I may be permitted to pass into a peaceful obscurity, with the hopes that their efforts may be more successful than mine.

This memoir was written in 1890. Mr. Denny lived more than eight years afterwards and during much of that time he took an active interest, not only in his own large business enterprises, but in all matters pertaining to the public welfare. For the last three years of his life, however, his failing health admonished him that his business affairs should be left to his sons who gradually assumed their direction and control.

Arthur Armstrong Denny

Personally, Mr. Denny was six feet in height, weighed about one hundred and seventy pounds, with no superflous flesh and was a typical specimen of the sturdy and stalwart sons of the West, who were prepared physically and intellectually to grapple successfully with any and all obstacles that might be encountered. Large in mind and body, with a moral character equally strong and well-developed, he continued to grow in the esteem and regard of his fellow citizens of Washington, from the time when he was elected a member of the Oregon Legislature in 1852—Washington being then a part of Oregon—until in 1897, when he was unanimously supported by the Republican members of the Washington Legislature for a seat in the United States Senate. He did not take his seat, however, or serve in the Oregon Legislature because the time required to obtain the returns from the large extent of territory he was elected to represent was so great that the term of the Legislature expired before he could be notified and thereafter reach the seat of government. In 1897 his party was in the minority in the Legislature, but these and many other incidents might be mentioned which illustrate the high esteem in which he was held by the people of Washington. In many respects Mr. Denny resembled Abraham Lincoln, not only in his personal appearance, but in his strong mental and moral characteristics, and in his keen perceptions of right and wrong, with the strength of will which enabled him to choose and follow the right, regardless of consequences.

Whilst in politics he was an earnest and consistent Republican, from the organization of that party, until his death, he yet enjoyed in an eminent degree the implicit confidence of all who knew him, without distinction of party, and his name was a synonym for honorable and upright dealing in public affairs as well as in private life. Identified from the beginning with the history of Seattle, his business enterprise and his high standing for commercial integrity did much to give to this city the favorable place which it occupies today in the financial centers of the world. For what he has done the citizens of the State owe him a debt of gratitude, and that debt could be discharged in no more satisfactory way than by studying his character, cherishing his memory and following his example. His acts of charity were numerous, but without ostentation, and one of his greatest pleasures was to afford relief to the needy, the helpless and the destitute.

In his domestic relations he was particularly fortunate. His life-long companion who became his wife nearly fifty-six years ago, and who was throughout that long period, his constant and trusted companion, adviser and a helpmate indeed, still survives him. From the time they began their long, toilsome and dangerous journey across the plains in 1851, until, after many years of hardship and privation on Puget Sound, they again enjoyed the blessings of civilization, she endured with bravery and patience all the trials of frontier life, incident to her situation, and thus, proved

18

herself worthy of a high place amongst the noble women of our country, who have rendered so much assistance in the work of laying the foundation of American Commonwealths.

Two daughters and four sons survive the happy union, all residing in Seattle. The daughters are: Mrs. Geo. F. Frye and Miss Lenora Denny. The sons are: Rollin H. Denny, Orrin O. Denny, Arthur W. Denny and Charles L. Denny, all prominent and highly respected business men of Seattle. Mr. Denny also left one sister, Miss S. L. Denny, residing in Seattle, and two brothers, David T. Denny, of Seattle, and A. W. Denny, of Salem, Oregon.

Mr. Denny left a large estate, chiefly in the City of Seattle, of which he was the principal founder, but his most valuable legacy was an unspotted character for loyalty and integrity and a long record of priceless and distinguished services rendered to the people of the State of Washington.

When he took his final departure he left behind him a noble example of

> "the high stern-featured beauty
> Of plain devotedness to duty.
> Steadfast and still, nor paid with mortal praise,
> But finding amplest recomplense,
> For Life's ungarlanded expense,
> In work done squarely and unwasted
> days."

WILLIAM F. PROSSER.

BISHOP BLANCHET.

FATHER DE SMET.

ARCHBISHOP BLANCHET.

FATHER BROUILLET

BISHOP DEMERS.

PIONEER CATHOLIC MISSIONARIES

Pioneer Days on Puget Sound

THE FOUNDING OF THE STATE OF WASHINGTON.

In these later days, when history is being made so rapidly, the following paper, which was read by the Hon. A.A. Denny before the State Historical Society, at a meeting held on the 31st day of May, 1892, will be found particularly interesting. It is a paper of great historical value, and especially so in view of the prominence which our State is fast acquiring, not only in the United States, but in the world at large because of its great natural resources and commercial possibilities. — Ed.

The first attempt at organized government in Oregon Territory was the provisional organization in 1843, and it might be remarked here that this organization did not include the territory north of the Columbia River. In 1852 active steps were taken to secure a division of Oregon and the formation of a separate Territorial government, which culminated in the holding of a convention at Monticello, an account of which I gave in an article in one of our local papers in March, 1889, and although it may seem like an oft-repeated story, in following the line I have marked out for this paper I must quote at some length from that article:

On November 25, 1852, a convention was held in Monticello, then one of the prominent towns of Northern Oregon, for the purpose of obtaining a division of the Territory. This convention framed and unanimously adopted a memorial to Congress, which was duly signed and forwarded to the delegate, Hon. Joseph Lane, a copy of which, with the names, is as follows:

To the Honorable the Senate and House of Representatives of the United States, in Congress Assembled: The memorial of the undersigned, delegates of the citizens of Northern Oregon, in convention assembled, respectfully represent to your honorable bodies that it is the earnest desire of your petitioners, and of said citizens, that all that portion of Oregon Territory lying north of the Columbia River and west of the great northern branch thereof, should be organized as a separate Territory under the name and style of the Territory of Columbia, urging these reasons:

In support of the prayer of this memorial, your petitions would respectfully urge the following, among many other reasons, viz.:

First — That the present Territory of Oregon contains an area of 341,000 square miles, and is entirely too large an extent of territory to be embraced within the limits of one State.

Second — That said Territory possesses a sea coast of 650 miles in extent; the country east of the Cascade Mountains is bound to that on the Coast by the strongest ties of interest; and, inasmuch as your petitioners believe that the Territory must inevitably be divided at no very distant day, they are of the opinion that it would be unjust that one state should possess so large a seaboard, to the exclusion of that of the interior.

Arthur Armstrong Denny

Third—The territory embraced within the boundaries of the proposed "Territory of Columbia," containing an area of about 32,000 square miles, is, in the opinion of your petitioners, about a fair and just medium of territorial extent to form one State.

Fourth—The proposed "Territory of Columbia" presents natural resources capable of supporting a population at least as large as that of any State in the Union possessing an equal extent of territory.

Fifth—Those portions of Oregon Territory lying respectively north and south of the Columbia River, must, from their geographical position, always rival each other in commercial advantages, and their respective citizens must, as they now are and always have been, be actuated by a spirit of opposition.

Sixth—The southern part of Oregon Territory, having a majority of voters, has controlled the Territorial Legislature, and Northern Oregon has never received any benefit from the appropriations made by Congress for said Territory, which were subject to the disposition of said Legislature.

Seventh—The seat of the Territorial Legislature is now situated, by the nearest practicable route, at a distance of 400 miles from a large portion of the citizens of Northern Oregon.

Eighth—A great part of the legislation suitable to the South is, for local reasons, opposed to the interests of the North, inasmuch as the south has a majority of votes, and representatives are always bound to reflect the will of their constituents, your petitioners can entertain no reasonable hopes that their legislative wants will ever be properly regarded under the present organization.

Ninth—Experience has, in the opinion of your petitioners, well established the principle, that in States having a moderate sized territory the wants of the people are more easily made known to their representatives; there is less danger of a conflict between sectional interests, and more prompt and adequate legislation can always be obtained.

In conclusion, your petitioners would respectfully represent that Northern Oregon, with its great natural resources, presenting such unparalleled inducements to immigrants and with its present large population constantly and rapidly increasing by immigration is of sufficient importance, in a national point of view, to merit the fostering care of Congress, and its interests are so numerous and so entirely distinct in their character, as to demand the attention of a separate and independent Legislature.

Wherefore your petitioners pray that your honorable bodies will, at an early day, pass a law organizing the district of country above described under a Territorial government, to be named the "Territory of Columbia."

Done in convention assembled at the town of Monticello, Oregon Territory, this 25th day of November, A.D. 1852

G.N. McConna, President of the Convention.
R.V. White, Secretary;

C.S. Hathaway.	C.C. Terry.
Q.A. Brooks.	J.N. Low.
A. Cook.	S. Plamondon.
E.H. Winslow.	A.J. Simmons.
A.F. Scott.	H.A. Goldsborough.
A.A. Denny.	M.T. Simmons.
William N. Bell.	H.C. Wilson.
G.B. Roberts.	L.B. Hastings.
L.M. Collins.	J. Fowler.

L.L. Davis.
N. Stone.
S.D. Ruddell.
C.H. Hale.
A.B. Dillenbaugh.
E.J. Allen.
D.S. Maynard.
J.R. Jackson.
William Plumb.
A. Wylie.
Seth Catlin
F.A. Clark.

B.C. Armstrong.
H.D. Huntington.
S.S. Ford.
A. Crawford.
W.A.L. McCorkle.
C.F. Porter.
N. Ostrander.
P.W. Crawford.
E.L. Ferrick.
S.P. Moses.
H. Miles.

The bill for the formation of Columbia Territory, in answer to this memorial, was earnestly supported by Delegate Lane, who, in advocating its passage in a speech in the house, said: "Aside from the seeming reflection upon the legislative department of the government of Oregon, and waiving what is therein represented as sectional strife between the people north and those south of the Columbia, I can scarcely hope to add to the causes set forth in this memorial, and to what I have already remarked in the expectation of influencing this house in favor of the passage of this bill."

On motion of Mr. Stanton, of Kentucky, the bill was amended by striking out the word "Columbia" and inserting "Washington" in lieu thereof. On February 10, 1853, the bill thus amended passed the house by a vote of 128 yeas to 29 nays, the nays by states being: Ohio, 2; Indiana, 1; Alabama, 5; North Carolina, 4; Tennessee, 4; South Carolina, 3; Georgia, 4; New York, 2; Virginia, 1; Louisiana, 1; Maryland and New Jersey, 1 each. On March 2nd the bill passed the senate without opposition.

Following the passage of this bill, in due time Isaac I. Stevens was appointed Governor and ex-officio Superintendent of Indian Affairs of Washington Territory, and was by the Secretary of War entrusted with an exploration and survey of a railroad from the headwaters of the Mississippi to Puget Sound.

I quote a letter in full from the Governor, which I received soon after his appointment:

Washington, D.C., April 18, 1853.

To A.A. Denny, Esq. — Dear Sir:

Herewith you will find a printed copy of my instructions from the Secretary of War, by which you will see an exploration and survey of a railroad from the headwaters of the Mississippi to Puget Sound is entrusted to me. To avoid the delay such expedition might occasion in the organization of the territory, Colonel Anderson, the marshal, will take a census preliminary to an election for members of the Legislature. He will be found to be a very worthy gentleman, and will consult with his fellow-citizens on all subjects of interest to the Territory, and for him and his brother officers I bespeak your good offices.

A military road is to be built from Fort Walla Walla to Puget Sound. Captain McClellan, an officer distinguished for his gallantry in Mexico, has command of the party who will make the exploration of the Cascade range and the construction of the military road. His undertaking the task is a sure guaranty of its accomplishment. I expect to pierce the Rocky Mountains, and this road is to be done in time for the fall's immigration, so that an open line of communication between the States and Sound will be made this year.

Desiring to know your views on these and kindred topics, inviting your consideration of the question of a proper location of the territorial capital, I am truly yours, etc.,

ISAAC I. STEVENS.

Though looking back over a period of nearly forty years, I think it will be readily discerned that from the time of the Monticello Convention, which framed the memorial already quoted, down to the organization of the first Legislature, was a most interesting to that time embracing our Indian war, I feel safe in saying that it excels by far in interest any period of like duration in our whole territorial life. But I have not the time and will not attempt to enter into a history of that period, except to a very limited extent. Colonel Anderson, on his arrival, proceeded with all possible dispatch to take the census, and found a total white population of 3,965. Upon the arrival of the Governor he made an apportionment for the first Legislature, and issued a proclamation on the 28th day of November, 1853, designating the 30th day of January, 1854, as the day for the first election of members of the Legislature, and the 27th day of February as the time, and Olympia as the place, of meeting. The Council was composed of nine members, as follows: Clark County, D.F. Bradford, William H. Tappan; Lewis and Pacific Counties, Seth Catlin, Henry Miles; Thurston County, D.R. Bigelow, B.F. Yantis; Pierce and King Counties, Lafayette Balch, G.N. McConaha; Jefferson and Island Counties, William P. Sayward.

The House consisted of eighteen members apportioned as follows:

Clark County—F.A. Chenoweth, Henry R. Crosbie, A.F. Bolan, John D. Biles and A.C. Lewes.

Island County—Samuel D. Howe.

Jefferson County—Daniel F. Brownfield.

King County—A.A. Denny.

Lewis County—H.D. Huntington and John R. Jackson.

Pacific County—John Scudder.

Pioneer Days on Puget Sound

Pierce County—H.C. Moseley, L.F. Thompson and John M. Chapman.

Thurston County—David Shelton, C.H. Hale, L.D. Durgin and Ira Ward, Jr.

Of that council, three survive, Messrs. Bigelow, Bradford and Tappan; and of the House, so far as I have been able to learn, all are gone but seven, Chenoweth, Brownfield, Chapman, Denny, Henness, Thompson and Shelton. This Legislature was composed mostly of young men—active, earnest and fairly well equipped to succeed in whatever they undertook. One of their first legislative acts was to call to their assistance, as a commission, the three judges of the district court, Lander, Monroe and Strong, to prepare a code of laws for the Territory, and it may be truly said that the work accomplished by that Legislature and assistant commission was highly creditable to all concerned.

At the time of the Monticello convention Thurston County embraced all of the territory north of Lewis County to the British line, and the session of the Oregon Legislature just prior to the division of the territory, formed out of Thurston County, Pierce, King, Island and Jefferson Counties in Washington Territory when organized, Clark County at that time extending east to the summit of the Rocky Mountains. The first session of the Legislature formed eight new counties.

Walla Walla was formed at this session embracing all the territory east of the mouth of the Deschutes River and running to the forty-ninth parallel on the north and the parallel of 46-30 eastward to the summit of the Rocky Mountains, and I well remember that a board of country officers was appointed, and representation in the Legislature provided for, but when the succeeding Legislature convened no members from Walla Walla appeared, and it was found that no organization of the country had been made for want of population, and the widely scattered condition of the few who then inhabited that vast territory.

Questions have often been asked, and very properly, too, as to the hopes and expectations of the early settlers. Forty-one years ago all of Puget Sound north of the mouth of Steilacoom Creek was as wild as when visited by Vancouver in 1792, but even when I expected to see a railroad from the Atlantic Coast to Puget Sound, and was only disappointed in the time of its accomplishment by the occurrence of certain events which were then not to be reasonably anticipated or foreseen.

When I located on the Sound it never occurred to me that the vast wilderness through which I had so recently passed, lying between the Missouri River and the Rocky Mountains, must be populated before the settlement of this territory, but such proved to be the case. Kansas and Nebraska Territories were organized and opened to settlement under circumstances peculiarly calculated to attract attention. The repeal of the Missouri compromise and declaration of the Douglas squatter sovereignty doctrine at once opened the question of slavery in the territories, producing a most bitter contest between North and South for supremacy in those territories. The effort between the two sections for supremacy was so great that it absorbed almost the entire moving population of the country. Very few during this whole contest found their way through that country, except the California gold seekers, a few of whom drifted northward and reached our territory, and I shall have to admit, although there are but few survivors to help me bear the responsibility, that we drew it rather strong in our Monticello memorial when we claimed "a large population constantly and rapidly increasing," but I think under the circumstances we should be excused, as we had so much room and were starting in to build an empire, we could not then see ourselves as others see us now. After we began to feel that we were really making substantial progress the Indian war of 1855 and '56 came upon us and spread ruin and desolation over our fair territory and a heavy percentage of our population were compelled to seek employment and home abroad, and very many of them never returned. Then came the great rebellion which paralyzed everything from the Atlantic to the Pacific, effectually checking all progress and improvement for a long period of time. Then, during all this period of slow growth, in fact, almost no growth at all, Oregon was our big sister, and, of course, must be first served, but I will do her the justice to admit that she was always willing that we should have what was left after she was served, and would try to help us get it, but we were thus, as it were, clad in cast-off clothes and dined at the second table, so that when I look back and recall our early experience I am not surprised that people now ask how we lived and what we saw in the future to encourage and inspire hope. Although we often experienced times of great trial and privation, at times almost in want of the necessaries of life, and the luxuries were not to be thought of or expected. As an illustration of the situation which possibly may be appreciated on the present occasion, I will mention one instance only. In the fall of 1851, Dr. William F. Tolmie sent me a large canoe load of potatoes from Fort Nisqually for my winter's supply, which were landed at Alki Point by Edward Huggins, one of your worthy citizens, then a very likely young man, who, if my memory serves me right, slept on the floor of my cabin over night, and if he was dissatisfied with his accommodations he had been too well brought up to complain in my hearing. I sometimes felt like reproaching myself for exposing my wife and children to such hardships and dangers as then surrounded us, but I never lost heart or hope nor regretted having cast my lot in Washington Territory.

There were forty-four who signed the Monticello memorial, and twenty-seven members of the first Legislature, in all seventy-one, and of that number I am not now able to tell how many are left, but certainly all except possibly fifteen have answered to the last roll call, and while it is a source of some pleasure to recall, and to write and speak of those early experiences and associations, it at the same time causes a feeling of inexpressible sadness, but I must not follow the subject further.

In conclusion, you will pardon me, I am sure, for claiming that those who blocked out Washington Territory, though it may have been roughly done, and conducted its affairs during the early period of its existence, did a good work and did it well. They laid the foundation for a State which is destined to take rank as one of the greatest in our grand and glorious Union of States.

A. A. DENNY.

REV. J.L. PARRISH.
Died 1895 in Salem, Oregon.

REV. A.F. WALLER.
8 May 1808—Dec. 26, 1872. Died of
heart disease in Salem, Oregon.
Married in 1833.

REV. DAVID LESLIE.
Died 1 March, 1869.

REV. GUSTAVUS HINES.
Died August, 1874.

REV. J.H. WILBUR.

PIONEER METHODIST MISSIONARIES

Pioneer Days on Puget Sound

PREFACE

THE INESTIMABLE value of a book such as Arthur A. Denny's *Pioneer Days on Puget Sound* can be best understood by those who have had occasion to examine early historical facts and dates in books of greater pretension. Scattered, turgid, often inaccurate, such is frequently the data relating to the Puget Sound country. Concise, clear, correct, is what students of Americana will observe Mr. Denny's book to be.

This little book is a thing with a soul. It makes its appeal as having some of the precious life blood of its author. Every old resident of Seattle loves it. It is not on record that a single copy of this exceedingly rare book has ever changed hands for money, — seldom for love, — so highly is it prized in its modest brown cloth covers of 1888. Should a copy of the original edition be offered for sale, there await a hundred collectors who covet it.

We have esteemed this reprint worthy of the most appropriate form and dress; worthy of being well printed, on good paper, with good black printer's ink, legibly, and, if possible, elegantly.

Seattle boasts but a scant showing in the literature of her local history, a fact that deserves comment when so many of her early settlers have passed away, leaving scarcely a line to record their part in the building of a great commonwealth.

In this brief yet eloquent record of pioneer days it is not difficult to read between the lines. These unpretentious annals give vivid impressions of patient, hard-working, loyal wives and mothers; of little children playing around log houses, on the shore, or on the wooded bluffs rising from the blue waters of the Sound; of friendly Indians, and, alas! others not so friendly; of long days of fear and nights of dread; of men who, venturing to the Land of the Tardy Sunset, worked and strove through the days when souls were tried. Some conquered; others fell in the hard, continuous struggle. All were heroes.

But beyond all, the author's splendid personality shines clearly, — his absolute integrity, gift of enthusiasm, energy, indomitable pluck and enduring belief in the future greatness of the city of which he was one of the founders.

No shaft of marble or tablet of bronze will perpetuate Arthur A. Denny's brilliant and never-to-be-forgotten services to Seattle as his "earnest endeavor to state nothing but facts." His memory will endure and be fondly cherished, his great work appreciated, long after the pioneers of Puget Sound have passed through the high stockade which Death places around Life, and found the end of the Long Trail to be the Land of Eternal Sunrise.

ALICE HARRIMAN.

29

HON. W.H. WALLACE,
STEILACOOM, W.T.

CAPT. WARREN GOVE,
STEILACOOM, W.T.

REV. JOHN F. DE VORE,
PIONEER METHODIST MINISTER
OF PUGET SOUND OF 1853.

DR. C.H. SPINNING,
TACOMA, W.T.

HON. W.R. DOWNEY,
STEILACOOM, W.T.

PIONEER DAYS ON PUGET SOUND

CHAPTER I.

From Illinois to Portland.

"Where arid plains extended
A toilsome way we wended."

IT IS NOW (1888) thirty-six years since I came to Puget Sound. I am more and more impressed with the fact as each succeeding year rolls by that the early settlers of the country will very shortly all have crossed over the river and be soon forgotten, for we may all concede the fact that we shall be missed but little when we are gone, and that little but a short time. But when we have met the last trial and our last camp fire has died out, some may desire a knowledge of such facts as we alone can give.

I shall therefore give a brief account of my removal to the Pacific Coast and my recollections of early settlements on the Sound, in which it will be my earnest endeavor to state nothing but facts. I shall confine myself largely to what I know personally to be true, and when I have occasion to speak of matters outside of my knowledge I shall, so far as possible, consult those who had personal knowledge of the facts stated.

No one person can be expected to get all the items or note all the circumstances that may be of some little interest to those who are to come after us, and I think it by no means improper for any of the few settlers now left, who may be so disposed, to contribute what they can to make up a record, which must now be very quickly done, if done at all.

The most important thing, in my estimation, is to make no wrong or incorrect statements. Let it be the pride of old settlers to state the truth. It is no time for romancing or painting fancy sketches when we are nearing the end of our voyage. The work is too serious for fiction. We want solid facts only.

We left our Illinois home on April 10, 1851, and crossed Iowa from Burlington to Kanesville, a Mormon town (now Council Bluffs,) on the Missouri river, traveling via New London, Mount Pleasant, Fairfield, Agency, Ottumwa, and Eddyville. We crossed the Missouri river on May 5th, and traveled up the north side of the Platte river, and passed Fort Laramie on Friday, June 6th. Estimated distance from Missouri

Arthur Armstrong Denny

river at 530 miles. On Saturday, the 21st of June, we crossed the summit of the South Pass. We reached Fort Hall on July 4th, distance estimated at 1,104 miles. From Fort Hall our line of travel was on the south side of Snake river. Saturday, the 5th, we camped a mile or two above American Falls, and on Sunday morning as we passed the falls we observed a large encampment of Indians on the opposite side of the river, and an armed party of eight or ten crossing just at the foot of the falls. This party came to the front of our little train, which at the time numbered only four wagons and seven men, and endeavored to induce us to stop, pretending that they wanted to trade, but we declined to halt. After we had passed them a short distance they fired, but on looking to the rear we could only see the puffs of smoke when they fired from behind the rocks. At the same time we could hear the bullets whistle and see the dust fly where they struck, but fortunately they did not hit any of us.

We now saw others crossing and running down the river toward the mouth of a ravine which we were approaching, but we succeeded in crossing and gained an advantageous position, where we halted and waited for them to come in range of our rifles. Seeing our advantage, they took good care to keep out of range. This was the only instance in which we encountered hostile Indians on the whole trip.

A few weeks later a family by the name of Clark, while traveling two or three miles ahead of the main train, were ambushed and massacred, as near as I could learn at the same ravine I have mentioned, and no doubt by the same band who attacked us.

On Monday, August 11, we arrived at The Dalles, and John N. Low, C. D. Boren and myself chartered a boat to take us and our families down the river, and sent our teams over the mountains by way of Barlow's Pass. We arrived in Portland Friday, August 22nd. The estimated distance from the Missouri river to The Dalles is 1,765 miles—eighty days' travel. Entire time, ninety-seven days, and to Portland, 108 days.

At this time all the western portion of Iowa was a very sparsely settled country, and after crossing the Missouri river it was without settlement to The Dalles, and there we found only traders' tents. The ground on which the Umatilla House now stands was then occupied by the tent of Wm. Craig, an Indian trader of note, and the boat which we chartered, belonging to a man by the name of Tudor, lay in the mouth of the creek a little west of that point.

At the Cascades we found the first houses which looked really like civilization. F. A. Chenoweth was building a tram road for the transfer of freight and passengers around the rapids, and at the upper landing were the Bradfords, Bush, and Bishop, with others not now remembered.* There was also a small side-wheel steamer, called

*These Bradfords were of the eighth generation from Governor William Bradford of the Mayflower, 1620. They built the "Flint."

the *"Flint,"* nearly completed, intended to run between the Cascades and The Dalles, which service she entered that fall. I do not now remember who built or owned her, but there can be no doubt of the fact that she was the first steamboat above the Cascades.

The navigation of that day between Portland and the Cascades differed somewhat from the present time. Chenoweth was running an old brig, called the *"Henry,"* no longer fit to go to sea, between Portland and the Cascades. Our baggage was the first freight to pass over the tram road and was taken over on a car by hand, while we made the trip on foot to the lower end of the rapids, where we boarded the brig and made the voyage to Portland by sail and the help of the current.

We found Portland quite a thriving town, probably containing a population of 2,000 or more even at that early period, giving promise of future greatness. It was reported at 821 inhabitants by the census of 1850, and in 1853 claimed 6,000 hence I do not think my estimate for 1851 can be far out of the way.

REV. J.S. GRIFFIN.

REV. C. EELLS, D.D.

REV. SAMUEL PARKER.

REV. E. WALKER.

REV. H.H. SPALDING.

PIONEER CONGREGATIONAL MISSIONARIES

Pioneer Days on Puget Sound

The Settlement on Alki Point.

"The beginnings of all things are small." — Cicero.

ON LEAVING HOME for what we called the Pacific Coast, we had no other purpose or expectation than to settle in the Willamette valley. But we met a man on Burnt river by the name of Brock, who lived near Oregon City and had come out expecting to meet some friends, failing in which he turned and came back with us to The Dalles. He gave us information in regard to Puget Sound, and called attention to the fact that it was about as near to the Sound from where we struck the Columbia river, now known as Umatilla Landing, as it was to Portland, but as yet there was no road over the mountains by which it could be reached.

My attention was thus turned to the Sound, and I formed the purpose of looking in that direction; but soon after our arrival in Portland my wife, one child and myself were taken with ague, which held us until late in the fall. This most effectually defeated all my plans for examination of the country.

In the month of September J. N. Low and my brother, D. T. Denny, drove Low's cattle over to Judge Ford's on the Chehalis river, for winter range, with the purpose also of examining the country. While awaiting a report from them I received a visit from Thomas M. Chambers, who gave me information which greatly increased my interest in the Sound country.

At Olympia they fell in with Lee Terry, and the three there joined Capt. Robert C. Fay and came down to the Duwamish river exploring. On the 25th of September they went up as far as where H. Van Asselt, L. M. Collins and Jacob Maple and Samuel Maple had shortly before determined to locate.

While looking around Low and Terry concluded to locate a townsite, and with that view made a joint location on Alki* Point. Low hired my brother to remain on the claim with Terry while he returned to Portland for his family, and on the 28th day of September Terry and my brother laid the foundation for the first cabin.

When Low returned to Portland the schooner *Exact*, Capt. Folger was fitting for a voyage to Queen Charlotte Island with gold prospectors, intending to touch at

*Pronounced Al-ke.

the Sound with emigrants. We determined to take passage on her. She sailed on the 5th of November, 1851, and cleared at Astoria, as shown by the custom house records, on the 7th.

We crossed out on the same day, and on Thursday, the 13th, our party, consisting of myself and family, John N. Low and family, C. D. Boren and family, Wm. N. Bell and family, and Charles C. Terry, landed at Alki Point. Added to these were my brother, David T. Denny, and Lee Terry, making in all twenty-four persons—twelve adults and twelve children—all at the present time (November 13, 1887), living but six.* The increase has been seventy-nine, all now living but six, making a total of 103 persons, and total number of deaths in thirty-six years, twelve.

Our first work was to provide shelter for the winter, and we finished the house begun by my brother and Lee Terry for J.N. Low. All took shelter in it from the rain, which was falling more or less every day, but we did not regard it with much concern and seldom lost any time on that account. We next built a log house for myself, which increased our room very materially and made all more comfortable.

We had now used up all the timber suitable for log houses which we could get at without a team, and we split cedar and built houses for Bell and Boren. These we considered quite fancy, but not so substantial as the log houses.

About the time we had completed our winter quarters the brig *"Leonesa,"* Capt. Daniel S. Howard, came to anchor in the bay. Seeing that the place was inhabited by whites, the captain came on shore seeking a cargo of piles, and we readily made a contract to load his vessel. We had no team at the time. Some of us went to work cutting the timber nearest to the water and rolled and hauled in by hand, while Lee Terry went up the Sound and obtained a yoke of oxen, which he drove on the beach from Puyallup, with which to complete the cargo; but we had made very considerable progress by hand before his arrival with the cattle.

Alki Point had not been a general camping place for the Indians, but soon after we landed and began clearing the ground for our buildings they commenced to congregate, and continued coming until we had over a thousand in our midst. Most of them remained all winter.

Some of them built their houses very near to ours, even on the ground we had cleared. Although they seemed very friendly toward us, we did not feel safe in objecting to their building thus near to us for fear of offending them, and it was very noticeable that they regarded their proximity to us as a protection against other Indians.

*Of the original twelve adults, Mrs. Mary A. Denny (widow of Arthur A. Denny), Mrs. Louisa Denny (widow of D. T. Denny and sister of Mrs. A. A. Denny and C. D. Boren), and C. D. Boren are living, in good health, February, 1908. Of the twelve children eight survive—Mrs. Louisa C. Denny Frye, M. Lenora Denny, Rolland H. Denny, Mrs. Olive Bell Stearns, Mrs. Virginia M. Bell Hall, Mrs. Mary Low Sinclair, Alonzo Low and Gertrude L. Boren.

PIONEER DAYS ON PUGET SOUND

From C. C. Terry's memorandum book.

30

Arthur Armstrong Denny

On one occasion during the winter Nelson came with a party of Green River and Muckilshoot Indians, and got into an altercation with John Kanim and the Snoqualmies. They met, and the opposing forces, amounting to thirty or forty on a side, drew up directly in front of Low's house, armed with Hudson Bay muskets, the two parties near enough together to have powder-burnt each other.

They were apparently in the act of opening fire, when we interposed and restored peace without bloodshed by my taking John Kanim away and keeping them apart until Nelson and his party left. He still lives, but John Kanim was killed years ago in a similar feud in Tulalip. However, it was not unusual for them to have a great war of words and no one hurt.

Col. G.O. Haller tells a good story which illustrates this point very well, of a difficulty occuring between two opposing parties on Whidby Island, in which he thought it was necessary to interpose to prevent bloodshed. He called on Tom Squiqui, who spoke English, to interpret for him, while he would talk to them and thus prevent violence. After he had spoken a few words, Tom exclaimed: "Don't be afraid, Major, they ain't going to shoot. You see, if Indian is going to shoot, he shoot before other fellow gets a chance and then talks."

Low and Lee Terry, as before stated, had located with a view of holding donation claims and laying off a town, which they did toward spring. The Terrys being New Yorkers, first named the place New York, but afterwards changed it to Alki, which all old settlers know signifies "by and by," "before long."

The object of all who came to Oregon in early times was to avail themselves of the privilege of a donation claim, and my opinion to-day is that every man and woman fully earned and merited all they got. But we have a small class of very small people here now who have no good word for the old settlers that so bravely met every danger and privation, and by hard toil acquired, and by careful economy saved, the means to make them comfortable during the decline of life. These, however, are degenerate scrubs, too cowardly to face the same dangers that our pioneer men and women did, and too lazy to perform an honest day's work if it would procure them a homestead in Paradise. They would want the day reduced to eight hours and board thrown in.

Pioneer Days on Puget Sound

Seattle Laid Off and Named.

"Now the work goes bravely on,"—Richard III.

TOWARD SPRING BELL, Boren and myself began to look for claims. We had looked up the coast toward Puyallup during the winter and did not like the prospect. In the month of February we began exploring around Elliott Bay, taking soundings and examining the timber. Piles and timber being the only dependence for support in the beginning, it was important to look well to the facilities for the business.

After a careful examination of the harbor, timber, and feed for stock, we, on the 15th of February, 1852, located and marked three claims in one body. The southern boundary we fixed on the point at what is now the head of Commercial street,* and on the north where Bell and D. T. Denny, who soon after located his claim, now join.**

We had left our stock in the Willamette valley to winter, and our plan was to get the stock over and then divide and move onto our claims.

On the 23rd of March the *Exact* came in on her return from the gold expedition, having failed to find anything of interest. Boren and my brother took passage on her to Olympia on their way to the valley for the stock, leaving Bell and myself in charge of the claims and families.

I am under the unpleasant necessity of again speaking of the inconvenience of illness, situated as we were. During the winter we did not shake with ague, but had not fully recovered, and before the return of the boys with the stock we were all down again, shaking every other day, and so continued until August. This was a very embarrassing situation for me, but I do not now remember that I ever felt particularly despondent or like giving up the struggle, for struggle it truly was.

On the 31st of March Dr. D.S. Maynard arrived at Alki in company with Seattle*** and a number of his tribe, who had been stopping at Olympia during the

*King Street and First Avenue South.
**First Avenue and Denny Way.
***In 1890 Mr. Denny gave the *Post-Intelligencer* a brief biography of Seattle:

"Chief Seattle was born at the 'Old Man's House,' on the present Port Madison reservation. His home was near Port Madison, but on the mainland. His father was a Suquampsh, his mother a Duwampsh. He was close to eighty when he died, as near as I can find out.

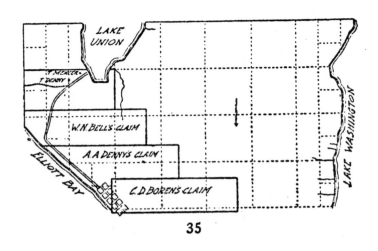

35

A. A. Denny
Donation Claim No 40 320 M

T 25 N R 4 E W M

114. 31
125.30

S 50°¾ E 409.5
31
S 38¼ E 17.67
21.29

63.80
32
27.12

28.90

68.63
26.38
04.70

60.20

winter. Their object was to establish a camp for fishing, and the Doctor was intending to pack salmon when the season for them came.

After an examination of the point, now called Milton.* and other places on the bay, they selected the southern point on our claims. Maynard at first declined to take a claim, stating that he only wanted a temporary location to pack fish for the season, but on further consideration he concluded to accept our offer and make a permanent location. We accordingly moved our boundary north to what is now the south line of Mill** Street in order to accommodate him with a claim.

On April 3, 1852, Bell, Boren's family and Maynard moved over, leaving myself and family too unwell to move until a house could be built.

Bell camped on the north and Boren on the south side of our territory until they could build cabins for themselves. They then built one for me on the bluff at the mouth of the gulch*** which runs to the bay in front of where the Bell Hotel now stands and moved us over. The front of our territory was so rough and broken as to render it almost uninhabitable at that early time. I dug a well forty feet deep in the bottom of the gulch and only got quicksand with a very limited amount of water.

Direct communication with the bay, by which we received all our supplies at that time, was next to impossible, owing to the height of the bluff, and I next built where Frye's Opera House**** now stands. We divided the territory so that each could have access to the water and made the claims as nearly equal as possible.

In October, 1852, H.L. Yesler arrived from Portland, looking for a location for a steam saw mill. He was pleased with the situation where Boren and Maynard joined, and as there had not yet been any claims filed in the land office, which at this time was in Oregon City, they each agreed to give him a portion of their territory in order that he might also obtain a claim.

These several adjustments were all amicably made, as all were anxious to enlarge the settlement as much as possible. The policy of laying off a town, and the name, had been discussed and agreed upon by us before Yesler came, which accounts for the fact that he does not appear as one of the proprietors in the first plat which was filed for record.

All had gone smoothly until the time when we (Boren, Maynard and myself) were to record a joint plat of the town of Seattle, when it was found that the Doctor,

"His disposition was not of the turbulent, aggressive kind, but rather of a mild and most generous type, with all the firmness and courage necessary to defend and maintain the rights of his people against unfriendly tribes. These traits, coupled with more than ordinary intelligence, gave him his influence among the Indians of the Sound and commanded the respect and friendship of the early settlers."

*West Seattle.
**Yesler Way.
***At intersection of Western Avenue and Battery Street.
****Northeast corner First Avenue and Marion Street.

who occasionally stimulated a little, had that day taken enough to cause him to feel that he was not only monarch of all he surveyed, but what Boren and I had surveyed as well.

Consequently Boren and I, on the 23rd day of May, 1853, filed the first plat of the town of Seattle. When, in the evening of the same day, his fever had subsided sufficiently, the Doctor filed his also. Thus it will be seen that the ground had been occupied for more than a year before the town was laid off.

Early in 1853 J.N. Low sold his interest at Alki Point to Chas. C. Terry and moved to the neighborhood of Olympia. Terry's brother having previously returned East, he thus became sole owner at the Point. On the 18th of April, 1855, he and Edward Lander* bought the front half of the Boren claim, and he soon after opened business in and became a resident of Seattle, and on July 11, 1857, exchanged his Alki property for a portion of the Maynard claim, and Maynard took up his residence at Alki.

*First Territorial Chief Justice, Washington made a Territory 1853.

Lots are 60 feet by 120, except Nos. 1, 3 & 4 of B. No. 1 & Lot No. 4 of B. No. 2 & Lot No. 0 of B. No. 0. & Streets and alleys are as represented on the above diagram. The above Town is laid out in the claims of C. D. Boren and A. A. Denny in King County, Washington Territory.

Seattle King County, W.T. May 23rd 1853
I H. L. Yesler Clerk of Probate do hereby certify that the above named C. D. Boren and A. A. Denny have this day been examined by me and acknowledged the above Town plat to be erect as laid out by them and of which they claim to be the proprietors

H L Yesler.

40

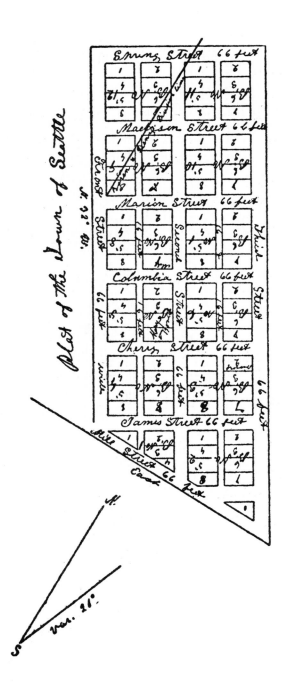

YESLER'S FIRST MILL, BUILT IN 1853.
This picture was made from a sketch drawn by **Mr. David Kellogg**, who clerked for **Mr. Yesler many years.**
The slab fire shown burned constantly where the **Totem Pole now stands in Pioneer Place.**
Plate XXIII.

Other Settlements.

"**Wings** that can bear me back to times
Which cannot come again;
Yet God forbid that I should lose
The echoes that remain." — Proctor.

HEN OUR PARTY landed at Alki, Olympia was quite a village, having been settled in 1847 by E. Sylvester. In 1851 Capt. Lafayette Balch located at Lower Steilacoom, and J. B. Webber and John M. Chapman at the upper town.

Of our emigrant party who came by the *Exact*, James Hughes and family settled at Steilacoom; H. H. Pinto and family and D. R. Bigelow at Olympia. John Alexander and family landed at Olympia, where they wintered, and in the spring of 1852 located on Whidby Island. Alford M. Miller, who was one of the *Exact's* party of gold prospectors, also located on Whidby Island, and H. H. Pinto crossed back and settled at Cowlitz Landing.

On the 16th of September, 1851, Henry Van Asselt, L.M. Collins, Jacob Maple and Samuel A. Maple selected claims on Duwamish river, and on the 27th of the month moved onto them from Nisqually river, where Collins had previously settled, and where, also, Wm. Packwood and George Shaser at the time were leaving, but I have not the exact date of their settlement on the Nisqually. There were of this pary in all seven persons, all now dead but Van Asselt. In the spring of 1851 A.A. Plummer and Charles Bachelor located at Port Townsend.

A few days after our party landed at Alki Point F.W. Pettygrove and L.B. Hastings came across from Portland and camped over night with us on their way to Port Townsend, where they made arrangements to locate. They returned and brought their families around on the schooner *"Mary Taylor,"* arriving, as I have been informed, on the 19th day of February, 1852.*

Of the other early settlers in the vicinity of Port Townsend now recalled were Albert Briggs, A.B. Robinson, J.G. Clinger, E.S. Fowler, John F. Tukey, J.J.H.

---

*The *"Mary Taylor"* left Portland early in the summer of 1852 with the first newspaper outfit north of the Columbia river, which was in charge of T.F. McElroy and James W. Wiley. This paper was issued at Olympia on Sept. 11, 1852, and called *The Columbian*. The plant used was the first plant of *The Oregonian*. It was taken to Portland from San Francisco in the fall of 1850, and the first issue of that paper (founded by Thomas J. Dryer, a strong Whig), was Dec. 4, 1850.

VanBokkelin, Thomas Hammond, R. Ross, H.C. Wilson, Henry Webber and James Keymes.

T.W. Glasgow told me of a settlement he made on Whidby Island in 1848, or possibly not till 1849, but owing to the threats made by the Indians he determined to vacate his claim, and in the fall of 1850 Col. Ebey located on or very near the place he had vacated.

Recently I received a letter from R.H. Lansdale, who came to Oregon in October, 1849, in which he gives a narrative of his early experience on the Sound, which I think worthy of preservation, and I shall give it in his own language:

"Reached Tumwater in January, 1851. Found Major Goldsborough at Simmon's and Col. Ebey at Olympia. Being advised by Ebey, started down Sound February 5th for Whidby Island, with King George, Duke of York, and Duke of Clarence.* Steilacoom was just then being settled, a vessel unloading at the time.

"Reached Port Townsend; saw immense Indian houses, but no settlers yet. Plummer not long after took his claim there.

"Crossed to Whidby Island and settled at Oak Harbor, February 10th. Made a good garden that year. Col. Ebey told me of Snoqualmie Falls, and I had Indians take me. Saw the Falls; prepared and walked—one Indian carrying baggage—to top of divide in Snoqualmie Pass. In the summer Asher Sargent landed horses at Oak Harbor for Wm. Wallace** and family, who settled at Crescent Harbor—so named by myself.

"I had now been many months alone, the few men being off helping to load piles for San Francisco wharves, so I fastened up cabin, potatoes, etc., and left to spend the winter at Olympia.

"As I approached Alki Point I saw a white man standing on the beach with a surveyor's staff in his hand looking to see who the white man approaching might be, and the man on the beach introduced himself as Arthur A. Denny.

"In March, 1852, helped to build a scow to take Crockett and Ebey's stock to Whidby Island. As soon as we landed I abandoned my claim on Oak Harbor on account of the mud flats, and took my claim at Penn's Cove. In 1851 there were three settlers at Oak Harbor, Martin Taftson, Clement W. Sumner and Ulric Friend."

In the spring of 1853 the brig *"Cabot,"* Capt. Dryden, came from Portland with quite a number of settlers for the Island. She made Penn's Cove by way of Deception Pass. Of those now recalled who came by her were James Buzby and family, Mrs. Maddocks and family, R.L. Doyle and wife, Mrs. Dr. J.C. Kellogg and family, the

---

*All Indians, who were hired to bring Dr. Lansdale down in their canoes.

**Colonel William H. Wallace, afterward sixth Territorial Governor (appointed by Lincoln in 1861) and, later, Governor of Idaho Territory.

Doctor having crossed by way of the Cowlitz, and Mrs. Smith and daughter, mother and sister of Dr. H.A. Smith.

It may be said with propriety that the settlement of the Sound below Olympia, or Budd's Inlet, by American citizens, began substantially in 1851.

This remark, of course, does not include the Puget Sound Agricultural Company's station at Fort Nisqually, and the Hudson Bay men connected with it, or even a few American citizens in the vicinity. At this time all white men were supposed to know each other, and their location and occupation, between the mouth of the Cowlitz river and Cape Flattery.

The man who had the best stock of health and the most faith and pluck was the most wealthy, for we were all capitalists in those days. Each one expected to help himself, and, as a rule, all went to work with energy to open up the country and make homes for themselves. At the same time they were ever ready to help each other in case of need or misfortune.

I will presume to say that if the people now possessed more of the spirit that then actuated the "old mossbacks," as some reproachfully style the old settlers, we would hear less about a conflict between labor and capital, which in truth is largely a conflict between labor and laziness. We had no eight hour, nor even ten hour, days then, and I never heard of anyone striking, not even an Indian. Every man who was worthy of the name (and I am proud to say that there were few exceptions then), was found striking squarely and determinedly at whatever obstacle stood in the way of his success. How unfortunate that it is not so now.

I confidently assert that for those coming to the Sound now there is a brighter future and a lighter task, if they will but lay hold in the right spirit, than there was for those who came in early times.

In 1853 we had quite an accession to our population on the Sound, from the immigration of that season, a number of whom came over the mountains by the Naches Pass.

In the fall of 1853 A.L. Porter located a claim on the prairie, which takes its name from him, and Dominick Corcoran and James Riley located on Muckilshoot prairie, the three being at the time the farthest out in that direction.

Lower down the valley were Wm. H. Brannan, Geo. King, Harvey Jones, Enos Cooper, Moses Kirkland, Wm. Cox, Joe and Arnold Lake, John M. Thomas, R.H. Beatty, and D.A. Neely.

At and near the juncture of White and Black rivers were Wm. H. Gilliam, Joseph Foster, Stephen Foster, A.F. Bryant, Charles E. Brownell, and further up Black river O.M. Eaton, Joseph Fanjoy, H.H. Tobin, and Dr. R.M. Bigelow.

Arthur Armstrong Denny

On the Dewampsh river, of those now remembered, who have not already been mentioned, we have John Buckley, August Hograve, George Holt, Dr. S.L. Grow, G.T. Grow, J.C. Avery, Eli B. Maple, C.C. Lewis, Bennett L. Johns.

On the lake John Harvey, E.A. Clark, T.D. Hinckley, Lemuel J. Holgate; on the bay south of town John C. Holgate, Edward Hanford, John J. Moss, and at the mouth of the river, Chas. Walker.

On the Puyallup were R.A. Finnell, Abiel Morrison and family, John Carson and family, J.W. McCarty and family, Isaac Woolery and family, Willis Boatman and family, Adam Benson, Daniel E. Lane, Wm. Kincaid and family, and others not now remembered — Nicholas Delin was located at the mouth of the river.

Pioneer Days on Puget Sound

The First Year in Seattle.

"The lofty oak from the small acorn grows."

HEN we selected our claims we had fears that the range for our stock would not afford them sufficient feed in the winter, and it was not possible at that time to provide feed for them, which caused us a good deal of anxiety.

From statements made by the Indians, which we could then but imperfectly understand, we were led to believe that there was prairie or grass lands to the northwest, where we might find feed in case of necessity. But we were too busy to explore until in December, 1852, when Bell, my brother and myself determined to look for the prairie.

It was slow and laborious traveling through the unbroken forest, and before we had gone far Bell gave out and returned home, leaving us to proceed alone. In the afternoon we unexpectedly came to a body of water, and at first thought we had inclined too far eastward and struck the lake, but on examination found it to be tidewater.

From our point of observation we could not see the outlet to the Sound. Our anxiety to learn more about it caused us to spend so much time that when we turned homeward it soon became so dark that we were compelled to camp for the night without dinner, supper or blankets. We came near being without fire also, as it had rained on us nearly all day and wet our matches so that we could only get fire by the flash of a rifle, which was exceedingly difficult to do under the circumstances.

Our camp was about midway between the mouth of the bay and the cove, and in the morning we made our way to the cove and took the beach for home.

Of course, our failing to return at night caused great anxiety at home. Soon after we got on the beach we met Bell coming on a hunt for us, and the thing of most interest to us just then was that he had his pockets filled with hard bread.

This was our first knowledge of Shilshole Bay, which we soon after fully explored and were ready to point new comers in that direction for locations.

The first to locate were Dr. H.A. Smith, Edmund Carr, E.M. Smithers, David Stanley, John Ross, F. McNatt, Joseph Overholts, Henry R. Pearce, Burley Pearce, and Wm. A. Strickler. McNatt and the Pearces afterward changed their locations, and Ira W. Utter and   Hall came in and occupied the ground at first held by them.

Some of them had the impression that the bay must be a great resort for salmon in their season and therefore named it Salmon Bay, but time proved it not to be a very appropriate name.

The narrative of our travels and discovery in this case will doubtless sound strange to some now, but it was not uncommon for inexperienced persons then to get lost between the bay and the lake, and in some cases it was necessary to look after them to prevent their suffering.

In April, 1853, Dexter Horton and Thomas Mercer arrived, and Mercer settled on the claim where he still lives.* He brought the first wagon to Seattle. At the time there was not a rod of road on which to run it, but we improved the trail so that the wagon could pass as far northward as his claim.

Of the early settlers in Seattle and vicinity now remembered who have not been mentioned as locating claims were Hillory Butler and wife, S.W. Russell and family, T.S. Russell, Robert Russell, Geo. F. Frye, George N. McConaha and family, Franklin Matthias, Henry Adams, William P. Smith and family, David Phillips, L.V. Wyckoff, S. Wetmore and family, M.D. Woodin, Ira Woodin, Walter Graham, John A. Chase, Wm. G. Latimer, Charles Plummer, Dr. J. Williamson, William Heebner, S.M. Holderness,** David Maurer, Robert Gardner, Jacob Wibens, Gideon Hubbard, Thomas Stewart, N.H. Ogelsbee, John Margrave, J.W. Margrave, Mrs. Conklin, George Bowker.

Of those on Whidby Island not otherwise mentioned were Robert Bailey, Capt. William Robertson and family, Walter Crockett, Sr., and family, John Crockett and family, Samuel Crockett, Walter Crockett, Jr., Charles Crockett, Hugh Crockett, Samuel Hancock and family, Henry McClurg, William and Benjamin Welcher, John Kinneth and family, J.S. Smith*** and family, Capt. Coupe and family, C.H. Ivins and family, John, Thomas, and James Davis, Jacob Ebey and family, Geo. W. Beam, Nathaniel D. Hill, Robert Hill, Humphrey Hill, William B. Engle, C.T. Terry and mother, Grove Terry and wife, George Kingsbury, Captain Barstow, Samuel Libby, Robert Hathaway, Thomas Cranney, Lawrence Grennan, Major Show and family, Isaac Power and family, S.D. Howe, R.B. Holbrook, G.W.L. Allen, Thomas Hasty and family, John Condry, J.Y. Sewell, Edward Barrington, Charles C. Phillips, Robert C. Fay, Thos, and Samuel Maylor, Caleb Miller and family, A.M. Miller, John M. Izett, James and Milton Mounts.

*Corner Roy and Taylor Streets.
**Had been a Portland merchant.
***Joseph Showalter Smith came to Whidby Island in 1853. After Washington was admitted as a Territory he was elected a member of the Legislature and unanimously chosen Speaker of the House. In 1857 he was appointed U.S. District Attorney by President Buchanan.

Pioneer Days on Puget Sound

Our first year on our claims (1852) was spent in building homes and getting out piles and timber as a means of support.

That year we were visited several times by the brig *Franklin Adams*, Capt. L.M. Felker, and about as regularly by the brig *John Davis*, owned and commanded first by Capt. Geo. Plummer and next by Capt. A. W. Pray. Each lumber vessel carried a stock of general merchandise, and upon them we depended largely for our supplies.

In the winter of 1852-53 but few vessels visited the Sound for several months, and as a consequence it was a time of great scarcity, amounting almost to distress.

Our pork and butter came around Cape Horn, and flour in barrels from Chili; sugar mostly from China in mats. That fall I paid $90 for two barrels of pork and $20 a barrel for flour.

I left one barrel of the pork on the beach in front of my cabin, as I supposed above high tide, until it was needed. Just about the time to roll it up and open it there came a high tide and heavy wind at night, and like the house that was built upon the sand it fell, or anyway it disappeared.

It was the last barrel of pork in what is now King County, and the loss of it was felt by the whole community to be a very serious matter. There were different theories about it. Some said it would float and had gone out to sea. Others thought it had rolled down by the action of the waves into deep water. We all turned out at low tide in the night with torches and searched the beach from the head of the bay to Smith's Cove, but the pork has not yet been heard from.

After the loss of the pork our flour and hard bread gave out. Fortunately we had a good supply of sugar, syrup, tea and coffee, and with fish and venison we got along quite well while we had potatoes. Finally they gave out.

We then had to make a canoe voyage to the Indian settlement on Black river to get a fresh stock of potatoes.

Flour sold as high as $40 a barrel. Finally the stock was exhausted so that it could not be had on the Sound at any price until the arrival of a vessel, which did not occur for six weeks or more.

This was the hardest experience our people ever had, but it demonstrated the fact that some substantial life-supporting food can always be obtained on Puget Sound, though it is hard for a civilized man to live without bread.

Type of Blockhouse.   Yesler's Cookhouse.   White Church and Parsonage.

Plate XXI.

Pioneer Days on Puget Sound

The First Saw Mills.

"And felled my forest woods." — Richard III.

THE FIRST STEAM saw mill* on the sound was Yesler's and when he began to cut lumber we built frame houses and vacated our log cabins as speedily as possible. I believe his cook house for the mill was the last log house in use in the place.

In the spring of 1853 J.J. Felt located at Appletree Cove and built a mill. After the first winter it was moved to Port Madison and afterward bought, enlarged and improved by G.A. Meigs.

Isaac Parker, Delos Waterman and S.B. Hinds came up on the brig *John Davis* to assist Felt in building at Appletree Cove, arriving in Seattle Feb. 9th, 1853, and began to work early in March. Also, in the spring of 1853, Capt. Wm. Renton came to Alki and built a mill, which, early in 1854, he moved to Port Orchard.

It now seems strange that men of such marked intelligence and experience as they possessed could have overlooked and passed by such superior locations as Madison and Blakely. I suppose it was on the theory that Puget Sound is all a harbor and it was not necessary to be particular, a mistake that has been made in many other cases on the Sound.

In July, 1853, Capt. William C. Talbot came to the Sound in command of the schooner *Julius Pringle* to select a site for a saw mill, in the interest of Wm. C. Talbot & Co. The firm was composed of himself and A.J. Pope, of San Francisco, Chas. Foster and Capt. J.P. Keller, of East Machias, Maine.

Among others on the schooner were Cyrus Walker, present manager of the Puget Mill Company, E.S. Brown, millright, Nathaniel Harmon, Hillman Harmon, David Foster, and James White, all of the State of Maine.

The cargo of the *Pringle* consisted of lumber, tools and supplies necessary for beginning the proposed enterprise.

They first anchored in Port Discovery Bay, from whence they made explorations around the Sound as far south as Commencement Bay. They finally determined to locate at Port Gamble, to which point the schooner was brought and discharged as soon as possible, and building commenced.

*Western end was near the northwest corner of Yesler Way and First Avenue South; eastern end extended across First Avenue South projected, and into Pioneer Place.

53

Arthur Armstrong Denny

On the 5th day of September, 1853, the schooner *L.P. Foster*, commanded by Capt. J.P. Keller, arrived, 154 days from Boston, having on board his wife and daughter, who were the first white women to land at Port Gamble.

The *Foster* brought the mill machinery and general outfit. After loading with piles at the head of the bay it was taken to San Francisco by Capt. Talbot. Capt. Keller remained in charge at the mill, where he continued as resident partner and manager until his death.

This trio of noble pioneers, Pope, Talbot and Keller, being now all dead, I think I may with propriety speak of their high character for business integrity and enterprise. They belonged to that class of men who do not idly wait for something to turn up, but were full of energy and push. They not only helped themselves, but were ever ready to extend a helping hand to the needy and unfortunate.

When Capt. Talbot and party were looking for a location they found Capt. Wm. P. Sayward and J.K. Thorndyke busily engaged in building a mill at Port Ludlow, which in time became one of the principal mills on the Sound. It has finally become the property of the Port Gamble or Puget Mill Company. Sayward, one of the founders, died recently in California, and Thorndyke, I think, is still living.

In 1853 Utsalady was located by Lawrence Grenan and two partners, Thompson and Campbell. In 1858 Thomas Cranney bought an interest. Under the firm name of Grennan & Cranney, they built a saw mill and operated it in connection with the shipment of spars to Europe, which was for a time their principal business. This mill has also become the property of the Puget Mill Company and is now one of the largest mills on the Sound. Mr. Grennan, one of the founders, died in 1869.

Seabeck was located in 1856 by a company composed of Messrs. William J. Adams and Marshall Blinn, of San Francisco, and J.R. Williamson, Hillman Harmon, and W.B. Sinclair, of the Sound. Work was commenced by Williamson in the fall of that year, and Blinn also came up the same fall with the bark *"Brontes,"* and in July, 1857, they began to cut lumber.

The first settler at Dungeness was Daniel F. Brownfield, in 1852, followed by B.J. Madison, J.C. Brown, Charles M. Bradshaw, Elliott Cline, John Thornton, Capt. E.H. McAlmon, Thomas Abernethy, John Bell, S.S. Erwin, John W. Donnell, G.H. Gerrish, Daniel Smalley, and some others not now remembered.

The first settlement on Bellingham Bay was in 1852, and those I now remember were Capt. Pattle, Henry Roeder, R.V. Peabody, Edward Eldridge, Daniel Harris, Capt. William Utter, A.M. Poe,* John Bennett and E.C. Fitzhugh.

*Editor Overland Press, Olympia, 1862.

The first settlement was made on the Snoqualmie river, on the prairie above the falls, by the Kellogg Brothers, in the spring of 1858, followed in the summer by J.W. Borst.

Their only means of transportation at that time was by canoe from Seattle, by way of the Sound and Snohomish river. There was not then a house to be seen on the whole voyage between Salmon Bay and their little settlement on the Snoqualmie.

In 1863 the first settlement was made in Squak valley by John Casto and wife, John Halsted, Frederick Johnston, James Bush and family, Wm. Dennis, J.P. Adams, Thomas Cherry, Nes Jacob Ohm, and L.B. Andrews and family.

Casto and his wife and Halsted were murdered by Snohomish Indians in revenge for the murder of some two or three of their people by a white man. As usual in such cases, the whites who lost their lives were in no way connected with the murder of the Indians. This circumstance, though not indicating a general hostile outbreak, had the effect to break up the settlement for a time.

The name Squak, or Squawk, as I should spell it, is a corruption of the Indian name Squowh, or, as some would think to hear the Indians speak it, might more properly be written Isquowh.

The tribe or band of Indians inhabiting Squak Lake and its outlet, numbering not more, probably, than two hundred when we settled on the bay, and now almost extinct, were Simumps, and not as some call them, Sammamish.

Duwamish, Snohomish and Suquamish are also all corruptions, and would more properly terminate in "psh," as Dewampsh, Suquampsh, etc.

MRS. A. A. DENNY (Mary A. Boren) and MISS LOUISA BOREN,
Afterwards Mrs. David T. Denny, in 1850. Miss Boren was the first
bride in Seattle; sometimes called the "Sweetbriar Bride."

Plate I.

Road Making.

"Measures back his way."—Homer.

UR FIRST EFFORT in anything like public road making was a county road from Steilacoom City to Seattle. Wm. N. Bell, L.M. Collins and John M. Chapman were appointed by the county commissioners' court, of Thurston County, Oregon Territory, as viewers. They reported on March 23, 1853, from which I quote as follows:

"From Seattle to Collins', on Dewampsh river; thence on the dividing ridge most of the way, striking the Puyallup river one mile above Adam Benson's claim; thence to crossing of Steilacoom creek, thence to Steilacoom, the terminus."

At the time this report was made Thurston County had no longer jurisdiction of the case, having been divided. The commissioners' court at the time of the division was composed of Sidney S. Ford, Sr., David Shelton and myself, and I retained and have since preserved this rather curious and now ancient document.

We, however, did not abandon the effort to get the road, but proceeded to open it by volunteer work, and also a road from Alki to intersect it near Collins'. These roads were traveled but little, and after the first year were allowed to go out of use for want of work to keep them open.

By act of Congress, approved Jan. 7th, 1853, an appropriation of $20,000 was made for a military road from Fort Steilacoom to Walla Walla. This money was expended under the superintendence of Capt. Geo. B. McClellan, of the regular army, afterwards Major General, in the year 1854, by the way of Naches Pass, and, as elsewhere stated, a number of emigrants came over in that season.

Our people at once turned their attention to opening a road from Seattle to intersect this military road, and practically accomplished it. By the next season it was found that the military road was not a success as a wagon road across the mountains. We next turned in the direction of the Snoqualmie Pass, so-called at the time, but it was what in later times has been called Cedar River Pass. It was in early times used by the Indians and Hudson Bay men as a pack trail, and was sometimes called by them Green River Pass.

This trail came over from Nisqually and crossed Cedar river well up that stream. It was intersected by another from Snoqualmie prairie, at what is now known as

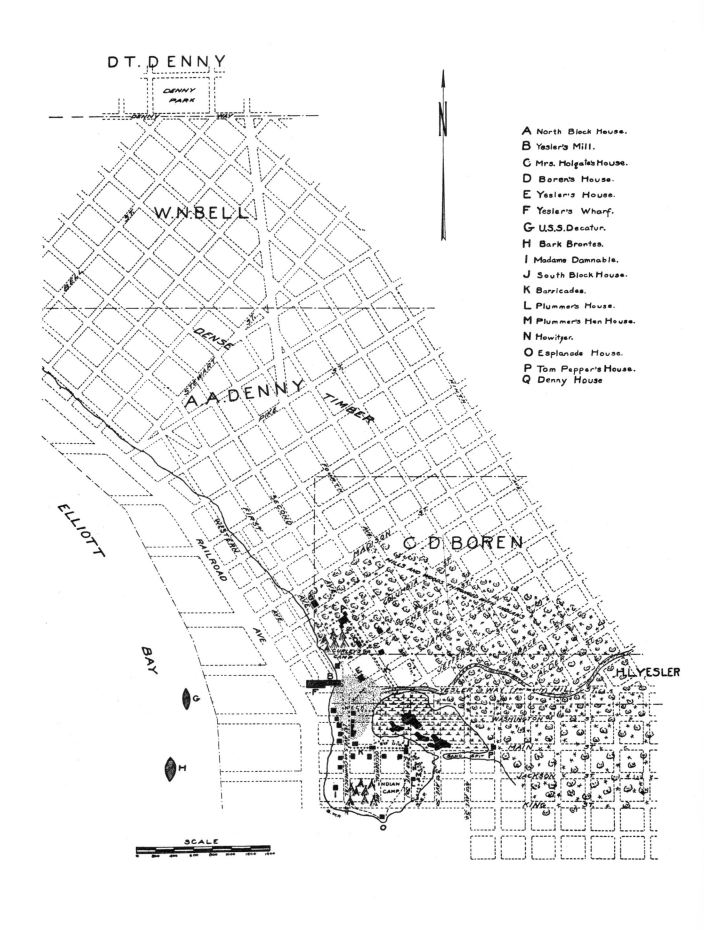

DT. DENNY

DENNY PARK

W. N. BELL

A. A. DENNY

C. D. BOREN

ELLIOTT

BAY

H. L. YESLER

A North Block House.
B Yesler's Mill.
C Mrs. Holgate's House.
D Boren's House.
E Yesler's House.
F Yesler's Wharf.
G U.S.S. Decatur.
H Bark Brontes.
I Madame Damnable.
J South Block House.
K Barricades.
L Plummer's House.
M Plummer's Hen House.
N Howitzer.
O Esplanade House.
P Tom Pepper's House.
Q Denny House

N

SCALE

"BEAVER," "DECATUR," "OTTER."

Plate XXV.

Rattlesnake prairie, and thence over the mountains to the foot of Lake Kitcheles, and thence down the Yakima.

There was another line sometimes used by the Indians, called the foot trail. It ran from the prairie up the south fork of the Snoqualmie to a point within about five miles of the pass, and then crossed over the divide to the west side of the lake. It was by this foot trail that Lieutenant Tinkham came over in February, 1854.

In the early summer of 1855 a party went out on a road expedition, composed of Judge Lander, Dexter Horton, F. Matthias, Chas. Plummer, C.D. Boren, A.F. Bryant, J.H. Nagle, Chas, Walker, Dr. Bieglow, and some others not now remembered. They went out by way of Squak and the Falls of Snoqualmie. Some of them went over the mountains by the foot trail to the lake, and others by the horse trail.

At one time they were camping at what is known as Rattlesnake prairie, and one of the party was startled by a rattling in the weeds. He reported that he heard a rattlesnake, which on investigation proved to be simply the dry seed pods of a weed; but it was sufficient to give a name to the place which it has ever after kept.

The party here again divided, some following the old trail over to Green river, and others down the Cedar.

As a result of this exploration we proceeded to cut a trail out by way of Meridian prairie, and thence crossing Cedar river at the old Green river trail and out by Rattlesnake prairie; but this trail was never traveled to any extent.

The Oregon Legislature, session of 1852-53, divided Thurston County forming on the north Pierce, King, Island, and Jefferson, and appointed as a county board for King, J.N. Low, L.M. Collins and myself, County Commissioners; H.L. Yesler, Clerk; and C.D. Boren, Sheriff. We all qualified except J.N. Low, and held the first commissioners' court March 5th, 1853.

We obtained our mail from Olympia, the nearest post office, by a canoe express, for which service we hired Robert W. Moxlie to make weekly trips between Seattle and Olympia.*

*This memorandum was made in C. C. Terry's note book before Seattle was named.

All were required to pay twenty-five cents a letter, and nearly all subscribed something in addition to support the express. For this service I gave the lot now owned by M.R. Maddocks, upon which the City Drug Store* now stands.

Our last express was received August 15th, 1853, and brought us twenty-two letters and fourteen newspapers.

August 27th, having been appointed postmaster, I received the first United States mail ever delivered in Seattle, and opened the office in a log cabin** where Frye's Opera House now stands. I, however, was not permitted to enjoy the distinguished honors and immense emoluments of the position long.

Dr. Maynard and two or three kindred spirits very secretly represented to the Department that I was not in sympathy with the administration; in fact, that I was not only a Whig, but an "offensive partisan," and got me relieved Oct. 11th, 1853, by the appointment of W.J. Wright, a little doctor.

This intrigue was discovered not long after the petition had gone on, and Geo. N. McConaha and other friends of the administration—in other words, Democrats— forwarded a protest. On May 4th, 1854, I was recommissioned by Horatio King, First Assistant Postmaster General, but I declined the appointment.

About this time Wright left the country, forgetting to pay his bills before starting, or settling with the Department, and Chas. Plummer was next appointed.

*Northwest corner of First Avenue and Madison Street.
**Northeast corner First Avenue and Marion Street.

CHARLES C. TERRY.
Born Sept. 20, 1829; died Feb. 17, 1867.

Plate XXIV.

HON. EDWARD LANDER.
Born Aug. 11, 1816; died Feb. 2, 1907.

Plate XXII.

Pioneer Days on Puget Sound

First Steamers, Churches and Schools.

"Such plain roofs as Piety could raise." — Pope.

IN early times we occasionally saw the Hudson Bay steamers, *"Beaver"* and *"Otter"** passing to and from the station at Nisqually, but as yet no American steamer had ever navigated these waters.

The first American steamboat was brought to the Sound by her owners, A.B., David, and Warren Gove, on the deck of the bark *Sarah Warren,* in October, 1853. She was a small sidewheeler called the *Fairy,* and made several trips to Seattle, and occasionally lower down the Sound, taking the place of our canoe express in carrying the mail. But she proved insufficient as a sea boat on the Lower Sound, and a small sloop called the *Sarah Stone* was for a time put on the line by Slater & Webber.

In the fall of 1854 James M. Hunt and John H. Scranton brought up the *Major Tompkins* and contracted to carry the mail on the Sound, running through to Victoria, and in March, 1855, she was wrecked in entering Victoria harbor.

The next steamer was the iron propeller *Traveler,* which came in the summer of 1855, and was commanded by Capt. J.G. Parker. Next was the *Water Lily,* a small side-wheel boat, brought up by Capt. Wm. Webster.

The fifth and last one I shall mention was the *Constitution,* put on by Hunt & Scranton to fill the place of the *Major Tompkins.*

The first religious service in Seattle was by Bishop Demers, a Catholic, in 1852.**

*The *Beaver* was the first steamer to enter the waters of the Pacific Ocean. Built in England in 1835, her launching was witnessed by King William, many of the nobility, and more than one hundred thousand people. But little was known of marine navigation at that time, and as the farewell salute of guns was given, her sailing away to the far-off Pacific Northwest was the occasion of much speculation as to the success of her cruise. So uncertain were the owners of her machinery that they had it placed in position, the side wheels not attached, and she was rigged as a brig, under canvas, for her trip. Captain Home in command.

The *Otter* was built in Blackwell, England, 1852. Her engines took first prize in the London Exhibition of 1851.

**"The Bishop's subject was "Charity," Miss Lenora Denny recalls. "I was a very little girl when I heard this, the first sermon I remember. But the speaker's earnestness impressed itself most vividly upon me ... he repeated his text often, saying, 'Charity, my friends, Charity.'"

Bishop Demers spent the night with A. A. Denny's family, and his genial, kindly ways are still a pleasant memory to Mrs. Denny and her children.

Right Rev. Modeste Demers was born in Eastern Canada in the early part of the nineteenth century. He came overland from St. Boniface, on the Red River of the North, to his first headquarters on the Pacific slope at Cowlitz and Nisqually, in 1838. He was the first Bishop of British Columbia, and died in Victoria, B.C., July 28, 1871.

The next was by Rev. Benjamin F. Close, a Methodist, who came to Olympia in the spring or early summer of 1853. He made several visits to Seattle during the summer and fall, and the same season Rev. J.F. DeVore located at Steilacoom.

C. D. Boren donated two lots for a Methodist Episcopal church,* and in November, 1853, Rev. D.E. Blaine and wife arrived** and Mr. Blaine at once engaged in the work of building a church on the lots donated by Boren. This church was dedicated in May, 1855.

This was the first and only church in the place until 1864, when Rev. Daniel Bagley built the Methodist Protestant church.*** He painted it brown, and, the other being white, they were ever afterward designated as the "White" church and "Brown" church.

Mrs. Blaine taught the first school in the same building used for a church; Miss Dorcas Phillips the second, and E.A. Clark the third.

These were not free schools, in fine and well-furnished houses, such as the youth of the place is now favored with. We were then glad to get schools at any cost and paid the expense without a murmer; but there is a vast difference now.

I am proud of the schools of Seattle to-day, where a high school education is furnished free to every child who chooses to take it. But I regret that it is in many cases so little appreciated by both parents and children that it almost justifies the expectation that the next step will be to pay the children for going to school, and allow them to strike for higher wages and shorter days, with the privilege of arbitrating the matter in the end.

The first Fourth of July celebration north of the Columbia River, of which I have any knowledge, was held at Olympia July 4th, 1852, on the hill, where the old schoolhouse stood, but it was then new and unfinished. Dr. Bigelow was orator, and B.F. Shaw, marshal, but I do not now remember who read the declaration.****

It was quite a respectable celebration, and was attended by most of the population within a day's travel, and quite a number, like myself, from a greater distance.

*Southeast corner Second Avenue and Cherry Street.

**David E. Blaine and Catherine Paine were married in Seneca Falls, N.Y., August 11, 1853, and took passage from New York for the Puget Sound country via the Isthmus of Panama, which they crossed on muleback. At San Francisco they were transferred to a sailing vessel bound for Olympia for a cargo of lumber. From Olympia they returned to Admiralty Inlet, arriving at Alki Point November 20th, 1853, and holding the first religious service at that place. The church was organized December 6, 1853. Services were held in a building situated near where First Avenue and Cherry Street now intersect. Mrs. Blaine began teaching the first school about January 1, 1854. Their first child, John, J. Blaine, was born January 20, 1856, and when three days old both he and his mother were carried aboard the *Decatur* to escape the dangers of the Indian outbreak. He is still living in Seattle. Rev. Mr. Blaine died November 23, 1900. Mrs. Blaine died March 9, 1908.

***Northwest corner Second Avenue and Madison Street.

****Benjamin Franklin Shaw came to Puget Sound (Tumwater) in the fall of 1845, and, with Col. M. T. Emmons and George Bush, built the first saw mill in the Puget Sound country. He was an excellent interpreter of the Chinook jargon and rendered most important service to Governor Stevens in his first treaties with the Indians. If his advice had been followed there would have been no Indian war. He died February 3, 1908.

Pioneer Days on Puget Sound

Those times we traveled almost entirely by canoe and never expected to make the trip from Seattle to Olympia in less than two days. In the winter I have frequently been three days, and camped on the beach at night, and on one trip—I well remember—in December, 1852, the weather was so stormy I had to camp two nights before reaching Steilacoom.

In after years I have paid as high as ten dollars steamer fare to Olympia, and when it got down to six dollars we thought it very reasonable. It always cost me more than that amount by canoe, when traveling alone with an Indian crew, to say nothing of the comfort and time saved by steamer, and time was quite as much of an object with us capitalists then as now.

We all had to make the time count—no time for standing round and finding fault because someone else had the best show, or strike for higher wages and expect some one to feed us while we were refusing to work, as now seems to be the case.

First Home on Alki Point. Built in 1851.

Plate III.

Pioneer Days on Puget Sound

Beginning of Indian Troubles.

"Treason and murder ever kept together."—Henry V.

URING THE FIRST two or three years after the settlement of the Sound fairly commenced the Indians were generally friendly, but in a few instances they committed murders when they thought it could be concealed.

A man with whom I was personally acquainted, by the name of Church, came to the Sound in the fall of 1851, and that winter went to Whidby Island, locating on Crescent Harbor, and was killed not long after by the Indians.

For this murder one Indian was convicted and executed at Penn's Cove. A surveyor by the name of Hunt was murdered on the Swinomish Slough, for which two Indians were convicted and hanged at Whatcom.

Another case which I remember was a man by the name of Young, who had hired Indians to take him down on the east side of Whidby Island in February, 1853. He was murdered by the two Indians he had in his employ. The murder was soon discovered and T.S. Russell, deputy sheriff, with a party of four white men and four Indians, went down to Holmes Harbor to arrest the murderers. This they succeeded in doing; but after getting them into their canoe, were fired upon by the Indians on shore.

One man, Dr. W.F. Cherry, was mortally wounded and died the next day, March 6th, 1853. The whites were all wounded, but none of them seriously, except Cherry. One of the prisoners was killed, the other escaped. One of the Indian crew was mortally wounded, and the other three escaped with injury. The whites claimed that they killed several of the hostile or attacking party.

There was also a white man killed in 1853, and buried on Lake Union,* near where the street railroad terminates at present. The Indians reported this murder, and the body was disinterred, but could not be identified. Two Indians were hanged for this murder without legal trial. Previous to this, in July, 1853, an Indian had been hanged for killing his kloochman, the same day he had committed the deed. Three persons—all now dead—were indicted for this offense, one of them was tried and acquitted, and the other two discharged without trial.

*Corner Eastlake Avenue and Valley Street.

67

Arthur Armstrong Denny

I have ever been opposed to mob law. It is a most dangerous method of punishing crime and settling grievances amongst civilized men, and where savages are concerned it is no better.

I have no doubt that two white men, one by the name of Rodgers, the other Phillips, were killed to compensate for the one Indian executed by the mob for killing his squaw. I think that it is safe to say that it has always been so in dealing with the frontier tribes.

If they commit crimes against the white and are dealt with and convicted under due process of law, I am very sure that the effect is much more likely to be salutary, and the penalty imposed accepted as a final settlement by the friends of the offenders.

I think this theory is justified by the result in the case of the two Snoqualmie Indians who were executed at Steilacoom barracks for killing Leander Wallace at Fort Nisqually in 1849.

On my arrival in the country, I early became acquainted with Pat Kanim, Chief of the Snoqualmies, from whom I learned the particulars of this case. He seemed to have a wholesome fear of the law and the power of the government and professed friendship for the whites. His sincerity he afterwards proved to the fullest extent; but the whites then in the country were disposed to look upon him and his tribe with distrust on account of their early trouble.

As early as the fall and winter of 1854, he gave me information of the growing dissatisfaction and feeling of hostility among the Indians east of the mountains.* By the spring of 1855, he showed such concern that I became convinced of his sincerity. I could see no motive but friendship, when he came to me privately in the night to warn me of approaching danger to the whites.

When he made his last visit and communication to me in the fall of 1855, shortly before the Indian outbreak, he stated that he was going up the Steilaguamish River to hunt mountain sheep, a circumstance to which I shall again refer.

In the summer of 1855, O.M. Eaton and Joseph Fanjoy crossed the mountains over the Cedar River trail on a mining expedition, followed not long after by a party composed of L.O. Merilet, J.C. Avery, Chas. Walker, —Jamieson and Eugene Barier.

After this last named party had reached a point in the Yakima Valley, near Simcoe, and while Jamieson and Walker were traveling a short distance in advance of the other three, they were shot down by Indians.

Fortunately those behind discovered what had happened in time to take to the brush and make their escape. They kept under cover during daylight and traveled by

*Indians east of the mountains were the real instigators of the war. They and the Snoqualmies came over and held war councils with the Sound Indians and urged them on to exterminate the whites.

68

night without trail or other guide than their own skill as woodsmen, and succeeded in reaching the settlement in a famishing condition.

The day before the return of this party Judge Lander, Hillory Butler and myself started for a trip, looking to an improvement of the road over the mountains. We camped at Black River, where we were to be joined by Dr. Bigelow, but when this party reached town and reported it, it was at once seen that the Indians east of the mountains were picking off all straggling parties. A messenger was sent to call us back, lest we should fall into a trap like Walker and Jamieson, and no doubt Eaton and Fanjoy before them, as they were never heard of after.

Shortly after this—date given by A.L. Porter, which I accept as correct, as September 27th, his house was attacked in the night; but he had been apprehensive of danger for some time, and adopted the policy of sleeping in the brush near by. When the attack was made on his house he at first thought it might be a party of whites wanting to stop for the night. He approached so near, in order to learn who it was, that he came very near failing to escape. Fortunately, however, he did escape, and warned the other settlers of the danger; thus warned, they came to Seattle for safety.

MISS L. GERTRUDE BOREN.

She was about three months old when the party started
across the plains.

Plate V.

Pioneer Days on Puget Sound

Indian Troubles Culminate — Seattle Attacked.

"Still from the sire the son shall hear of the stern strife." — Scott.

T THIS TIME THE sloop of war *"Decatur,"* Capt. Isaac S. Sterrett, came to anchor in the harbor.* We at once made a statement to him of our exposed situation, and a request for protection. This he promptly promised to give.

Gov. Stevens had but recently made treaties with all the Indians on the Sound, and in the Yakima country. He was, at this time, in the Bitter Root country, not aware of what was transpiring behind him. In fact, he was not suspecting any treachery or bad faith on the part of the tribes he had so recently treated with.

It was also most unfortunate that those having charge in his absence were not calculated to deal understandingly with the Indians. They refused to believe that there was any danger until the outbreak came, when in fact there was abundant evidence of the impending danger.

When Acting Gov. Mason heard that Porter's house had been attacked, and that through his escape and warning, the settlers on the Upper White River had left their homes and come to Seattle for safety and were engaged in building block houses, he took Lieutenant Nugent, with a squad of soldiers from Steilacoom barracks, and went out by way of Puyalup to Muckilshoot and Porter's Prairie and had a talk with the Indians. The Indians succeeded in deceiving him by professing friendship for the whites, telling him that they were foolish for leaving and ought to come back.

He came down White River by canoe to Seattle, and told the people they ought to return to their homes at once, and were perfectly safe in doing so.

He then went on board of the *Decatur* and made the same report to Captain Sterrett. He told him that it was all a false alarm, and that he might with perfect propriety leave at any time. He also, without delay, departed for Olympia himself.

Capt. Sterrett at once concluded that he had been victimized by a set of land sharks for purposes of trade, and singled me out as one of the chief offenders.

*The *Decatur* was one of three sister sloops — *Yorktown*, *Marion*, and *Decatur*.

71

The first Postoffice in Seattle—built in the winter of 1852-53.

Plate VI.

CHIEF SEATTLE.
Died June 7, 1866.

Plate VIII.

OLIVE J. BELL STEARNS, LAURA K. BELL COFFMAN,
MARY VIRGINIA BELL HALL.

Plate VII.

Arthur Armstrong Denny

He accordingly came on shore as soon as Mason and Nugent had left, and called on me. In a very heated manner he stated what Mason had said; that he felt that he had been grossly deceived and imposed upon by us, and that he would immediately get his ship under way and leave.

I replied that Mason, and those to whom we had a right to look for protection, were deceived, and that Mason had now deceived him; but if he chose to believe Mason and desert us to time of extreme danger, I had no power to prevent his doing so. Further, if our people, who were then here in safety, were induced by Mason's advice, to return to their homes, they would be murdered within a fortnight.

After reflecting a short time, he remarked: "How can I tell whom to believe; you seem to be so earnest I will stay and find out for myself."

Some of us tried to induce those who were here to stay; but a number of them came to the conclusion that Porter was alarmed without cause, and that Mason ought to know best and must be right, and so returned to their homes.

It may now seem strange that there could have been any doubt of the true situation, when it is remembered that the fact was known to all, that Walker and Jamieson had been killed, and that Eaton and Fanjoy were missing. There was no reason to doubt that they had shared the same fate. Yet many of the citizens were ready to agree with Mason, and ridicule those who had given timely warning, calling them timid and even cowards.

Within the time I had predicted to Capt. Sterrett the outbreak came, and on the 28th of October, 1855, Wm. H. Brannan, wife and child; Harvey K. Jones and wife, Geo. E. King and wife and Enos Cooper were killed, and an infant child of King's could not be found. Whether the babe was killed or carried off will never be known certainly, though there is reason to believe that it was killed and burnt in the house.

The settlers lower down the valley narrowly escaped and succeeded in again reaching Seattle in safety. The consternation and alarm was now general. None could be found to doubt the fact that the Indians were unfriendly. Those who, a short time before, insisted that the Indians were all friendly, would now declare most vehemently that all were hostile, and must all be treated as enemies.

Immediately after the White River massacre, Lieut. Slaughter was ordered up the old military road, to the Naches Pass. After reaching Porter's Prairie, he sent down an express to Gov. Mason, stating that Pat Kanim was dogging him at every step, and around his camp every night.

On receipt of this dispatch, Mason sent an express to Capt. Sterret at Seattle, instructing him to immediately arrest two of Pat Kanim's brothers, with all members of the tribe who were then camping in Seattle, and put them in irons.

Pioneer Days on Puget Sound

Having previously stated to Capt. Sterrett that I had received information from Pat Kanim that convinced me of his friendship and that of his tribe, the Captain did not feel willing to take so important a step without consultation. He sent for me to come on board the *Decatur*, when he stated what he was directed to do. He said that he must make the arrest at once, for the Snoqualmies would certainly leave during the night.

This was startling news to me. I most earnestly protested, telling him that I knew Lieutenant Slaughter was mistaken, and that we had enemies enough to look after without attacking our friends. But he was so much disposed to act on Gov. Mason's orders that I finally proposed, if he would not disturb the Snoqualmies, I would prove to him that Slaughter was wrong, by going to Pat Kanim's camp and bringing him in.

He very positively refused to allow me to leave town, but consented that I might send an express for Pat Kanim, and stand responsible for them until their return. A time was agreed upon within which they would be back.

Very fortunately for me, and probably for Pat Kanim, too, he was on hand within the time agreed upon. He had his women and children with him. He also brought a cargo of mountain sheep, venison, horns and hides, specimens of which he took on board and presented to the Captain.* Capt. Sterrett expressed the greatest surprise and satisfaction with the conclusive proof, which I had thus furnished, of the good faith and friendship of the Snoqualmies.

I never heard anything more from headquarters of the hostile Snoqualmies, but Pat Kanim was very soon employed by the Governor with a party of his tribe as scouts, and did good service during the continuance of the war.

Now to refer again to the evil effects which have always, in my opinion, followed any attempt to punish Indians by mob violence, as was done here in the case cited before, in which two white men were secretly made way with. I think the case of the Snoqualmies furnishes the strongest proof, that the effect is very different, where they can see that there is careful, dispassionate investigation, followed by punishment for the wrong committed.

Pat Kanim and his brothers gave me the particulars of their case, as I have before stated. They professed to accept the judgment of the court as just, and expressed a wish to cultivate friendship with the whites, and I think we have conclusive evidence of the sincerity of their professions, in that they were ever afterwards the friends of the whites.

I will say further, that my acquaintance and experience with the Puget Sound Indians proved them to be sincere in their friendship, and no more unfaithful and

*Capt. Sterrett was placed on the furlough list and relieved by Capt. Gansevoort in December, 1855.

treasonable than the average white man. I am disposed to believe that the same might be truthfully said of many other Indians.

After the White River massacre it was determined to prepare for defense in case of an attack on the town. At the time there was a large amount of hewn timber on hand twelve inches square, which was well suited to the purpose.

Two houses were built of this timber, of sufficient capacity to hold the entire population at the time. One was located at the junction of Front* and Cherry Streets, and the other at the junction of Main Street and South Second Avenue. The two were joined by a stockade, which also ran from each blockhouse westward to the bay, and was well calculated for protection on the land side of the town, from whence all attacks were likely to come.

Early in the morning of January 26th, 1856, the town was attacked by the Indians. They had congregated during the night and taken their position under cover of the timber, along the face of the hill, in readiness to make the attack as soon as the people began to stir. Their presence was made known by friendly Indians before the attack was made. A howitzer was fired by order of Capt. Gansevoort in the direction indicated by the friendly Indians. This was promptly followed by an answer of musketry all along the woods in rear of the town, and fully demonstrated the fact that the place was really surrounded by the hostiles.

Fortunately all the whites who were sleeping outside of the stockade escaped to the blockhouses without injury. The firing was kept up all day and two whites were killed. One was Robert Wilson, who fell near the southern blockhouse; and the other, Milton G. Holgate, brother of Mrs. E. Hanford and Lemuel J. Holgate, who still reside among us, was shot while standing in the door of the Cherry Street blockhouse.

The two houses were burnt during the day, one near where the gas works now are,** and the other the dwelling of Mr. Bell.*** Several other houses, my own among the number, were plundered during the evening, and everything of value carried off.

It is a mere matter of opinic... ...ether the town without the aid of the *Decatur* would have been able to withstand the attack; but with the help of the marines on shore and the guns of the *Decatur* in the harbor it was quite a different matter.

*First Avenue and Cherry Street, and the other at the junction of Main Street and Occidental Avenue.

**Fourth Avenue South and Jackson Street.

***Not far from Battery Street and Western Avenue.

From '56 to '67.

"So ends the bloody business." — Odessy.

OLLOWING THE White River massacre the upper valley had been laid waste. As the hostiles withdrew from the attack on the town they completed the work of destruction. With the exception of Alki, which was out of their range and escaped destruction, I do not think there was a house left standing outside of the present limits of the town. There were two or three that had been fired and not entirely destroyed.

King County, at the commencement of hostilities, was in a fairly prosperous condition, but now all was in ruins. The entire population was compelled to seek shelter and safety in Seattle or elsewhere, and a great many were so discouraged that they left the country.

The war continued until the fall of 1856, but I do not propose to follow the subject farther, as the principal incidents of the struggle are matters of historical record already.

I will say, however, that under protection of a company of volunteers there was sufficient ground cultivated in the lower valley to supply the few families that remained with vegetables for the next winter. Those were times of pinching want and great privation, such as we never experienced here except in the winter of 1852-3.

Those who remained until the close of the war were so discouraged, and so much in dread of another outbreak, that they were unwilling to return to their homes in the country and undertake the task of rebuilding them. As a consequence it was years before we recovered our lost ground to any great extent.

Business was generally stagnant. Little in the way of building or improvement was attempted. Roads that had been opened before the war had mostly become well nigh impassable, and some of them entirely so. Active efforts were not resumed to improve our roads and open communication with the country east of the mountains until 1865, a period of ten years.

In August, 1865, J. W. Borst, Wm. Perkins and myself determined to make a trip over the Snoqualmie Pass proper, for the purpose of finding a more favorable line for a wagon road than that by the Cedar River pack trail.

77

Arthur Armstrong Denny

At the time we could only find one Indian chief (Saniwa)* who had ever been through. He stated that it was lower than where the trail crossed, and was hard to get through on account of brush and timber, but was good for a wagon road.

He would not undertake the trip, but gave directions to two young Indians, who took us up the foot trail, with which they were acquainted. They pointed out the line of Lieut. Tinkham's travels and other whites who had crossed since; but from that point through the pass where the road now runs to near the head of the lake it was a trackless wilderness, over which the Indians had not traveled except on rare occasions. In fact, going down by the east side of the lake made a distance of at least fifteen miles of unexplored country.

On this trip we left Borst's on August 13th, and made our first camp at about nine miles, on the river bank. On the 14th, at about twenty-four miles, we left the foot trail, and at 5 o'clock camped on the river.

The 15th, at about twenty-nine miles from Borst's, by our estimate, we crossed the summit. About nine miles from the summit we reached the trail near the foot of the lake, where we found John Ross, L. V. Wyckoff and Saniwa camped with our horses awaiting our arrival.

I am aware that it is understood by some that Tinkham and others had been over the same ground before, but I know from the statement of the Indians and from our own observations that such is not the fact.

From the camp at the foot of the lake Borst, Perkins and the Indians returned, and Wyckoff, Ross and myself proceeded down the valley to the old military road, and returned over the Naches Pass.** At this time there was not a white person to be seen on the whole line of our travels until we reached White River at Thomas' place.

On our return a party was organized to commence work immediately, under the superintendence of Perkins, to open a road through the pass by the line which we had explored. They reached a point that fall about fifteen miles above Borst's, where work was suspended for the winter, but was not resumed the next season.

In the summer of 1867 we again took up the work where Perkins left off and opened the road to a connection with the Cedar River pack trail at the foot of Lake Kitcheles.

Thus at last, after years of effort, was accomplished a work which had been a favorite enterprise with the people of the middle Sound from its first settlement. The road was far from good, but it was at the time a great work, considering the means available to accomplish it, and, though poor, it served to open up direct communication with the country east of the mountains.

*Chief Saniwa was a very dignified Indian—small, but very erect, with an exalted idea of his own importance. He was a Klickitat.

**Official spelling U.S. Board on geographical names.

This work mainly devolved upon and was accomplished by the people of King County. If the Territory at large could have seen its importance in the true light this would not have been so, but it would have been improved and early made a general thoroughfare to the great benefit of both sections of the Territory.

DAVID T. DENNY.
Born March 17, 1832; died Nov. 25, 1903.

Plate IV.

LOUISA C., M. LENORA, ROLLAND H., and ORION O. DENNY.
Rolland was born in Portland, Sept. 2, 1851, less than two weeks after
the party arrived in Oregon. Orion O. was the
Plate II.   first white boy born in Seattle.

Pioneer Days on Puget Sound

Miscellaneous.

"They gained what such life alone can give:
The lore of men that ha' dealt with men
In the new and naked lands."

URING MY RESIDENCE in this country I have endeavored to avoid making statements, either verbal or written, that would be misleading to those who were looking to this Coast with a view of coming here to settle. I never yet advised any one to come, believing that the only proper thing is for each one to take the whole responsibility of determining for themselves.

All old settlers know that it is a common occurrence for parties who have reached here by the easy method of steamer or railway in a palace car, to be most blindly unreasonable in their fault finding. They are often not content with abusing the country and climate, but they heap curses and abuse on those who came before them by the good old method of from four to seven months crossing the plains, just as though we had sent for them and thus given them an undoubted right to abuse us for their lack of good, strong sense.

Then we all know, too, that it has been a common occurrence for those same fault-finders to leave, declaring that the country was not fit for civilized people to live in. It is not by any means unusual for the same parties to return after a short time ready to settle down and commence praising the country and climate as though they wanted to make amends for their unreasonable behavior in the first instance.

I regret that we have no connected and reliable record of rainfall and temperature from the first settlement of the Sound. Where it is necessary to depend upon memory I have found that great mistakes are made and matters get badly mixed.

It is very common, as we all know, to hear people complaining of the weather, asserting that it is the coldest or the hottest, the wettest or the dryest they ever saw without seeming to think how reckless and misleading such expressions are.

Then the "oldest inhabitant" so often confidently states that this is the coldest winter ever known. The news reporter interviews him, and out comes the announcement: "Coldest winter on record," with probably the information that the climate has greatly changed since the first settlement of the country. Very likely

81

reasons are assigned for the change, when, in fact, if we had a record of rainfall and temperature for the time covered by the memory of the oldest inhabitant, and his father before him, we would find that things had remained substantially as they were ages before.

I will, however, take the risk myself of making some statements in regard to our Puget Sound climate, which must be based largely on recollection or memory.

The winter of 1851-2 being my first in the country, I would very naturally have a more distinct recollection of it than of succeeding winters, and I can confidently say that it was quite a mild winter. We had but little snow and no freezing to speak of, and ice not more than half an inch in thickness.

The winter of 1852-3 was one of our coldest, but I had the misfortune to break my thermometer before it got the coldest, and I could not replace it, and cannot, therefore, give the temperature.*

We had a twelve-inch snow on the bay, and I was informed that it was much deeper at the head of the Sound. The snow remained on the ground two or three weeks. Ice formed on the mud flats and mouth of the river, and floated back and forth with the tide so as to seriously interfere with boats and canoes crossing the bay. There would be several hours during flood tide when the ice would be packed up toward the mouth of the river that the bay was clear, the obstruction occurring again with the ebb.

The coldest winter we ever experienced on the Sound was 1861-2. I then carefully observed my thermometer, and the lowest point reached by my observation was two degrees below zero. I have never known it lower than that at any time.

It should be remembered that the amount, or thickness of ice formed, does not depend so much on the actual degree of cold as on the duration of freezing weather. I think this fact accounts, to some extent, for the different estimates we get of cold weather when not based on instrumental observation. Then there may be a difference of several degrees in thermometers, and quite as much in location or exposure; hence we have contradictory reports.

Of late years I have kept several thermometers by different makers, and have compared them carefully to be sure that there was no great error in the instrument. With this preparation and a northern exposure, I have noted the following as the coldest days for the last three winters:

February 11, 1884, 6 degrees above zero.

December 30, 1885, 10 degrees above zero.

*Mr. George H. Hines, of the Oregon Pioneer Association and Assistant Secretary of the Oregon Historical Society, a friend of Mr. Denny's for a great many years, who began keeping a diary at Olympia on October 1, 1858, and has almost a perfect record up to the present time (February, 1908), testifies to the correctness of his observations upon the weather.

Pioneer Days on Puget Sound

January 17, 1886, 14 degrees above zero.

February 4 and 5, 1887, 10 degrees above zero.

The heaviest wind storm since the settlement of the country was on the night of November 16, 1875. This was simply a strong gale which threw down considerable timber and overturned light structures, such as sheds and out buildings.

It is safe to assume that there has not been a hurricane or cyclone on the Sound or west of the Cascade mountains for ages, if ever. There are no marks to indicate it anywhere in the timber. The marks and course of a hurricane could be plainly seen and traced in the timber of this country for hundreds of years.

The deepest snow ever known here was in January, 1880, measuring four feet and a half after it had settled, and would have measured much more as it fell. I made inquiry of the Indians and could get no account of anything like it before. It may therefore safely be called unusual, as the like has not been known to the white inhabitants except in this instance.

In closing I will say that it was not my purpose to come down to a late date in this sketch, but to confine myself to the very earliest settlements on the Sound. I have not to any extent spoken of settlements at the head of the Sound and beyond it, for reason that they antedate my time. I therefore thought it proper to leave that duty to some one who could to a great extent speak from personal knowledge.

Some may also think that I have omitted names which should have been mentioned. To this I will say I have doubtless failed to recall some who were here in earliest times. Where I have spoken of families I did not think it necessary to name all the members of each family. Also, there is a large number who rank as old settlers, and who are worthy of honorable mention at all times, but do not come within the time properly covered by these notes.

I hope some one who is better qualified than myself will take up the history where I now leave it.

MR. A. J. CHAMBERS, MRS. A. A. DENNY, MR. C. D. BOREN,
Crossed the Plains.
1845.   1851.   1851.
Picture taken August, 1907.

Plate XXXII.

ARTHUR A. DENNY, ROLLAND H. DENNY, EDITH DENNY
LAMPING, ROLLAND DENNY LAMPING.
Plate XXXIV.

CHRONOLOGICAL NOTES

Of the early settlement of that part of
Washington Territory now em-
braced principally in
King County

16th of September, 1851, Henry Van Asselt, Jacob Maple, Samuel Maple and L. M. Collins selected claims on Duwamish river, and on the 27th of the month moved on to them from the Nisqually river, where Collins had previously located.

On the 25th or 26th of September, 1851, John N. Low, Lee Terry and David T. Denny arrived at Alki Point, where Low and Terry located a claim, and on the 28th of September Terry and Denny laid the foundation for the first house on the claim, Low having returned to Portland for his family.

5th of November, 1851, the schooner *Exact*, Captain Folger, sailed from Portland for Puget Sound and Queen Charlotte's Island, with passengers for the Sound and a party of gold miners for the island.

13th of November she arrived at Alki Point and landed J. N. Low, Wm. N. Bell, C. D. Boren and A. A. Denny, with their families.

15th of February, 1852, Bell, Boren and A. A. Denny located claims on the east side of Elliott's Bay, extending north from what is now the head of Commercial Street to Bell's present northern boundary, and on the 23rd of March Boren and D. T. Denny started to the Willamette valley for the stock, leaving Bell and A. A. Denny to look after the claims till their return.

31st of March, 1852, Dr. D. S. Maynard arrived at Alki Point, and Bell and Denny agreed to move their southern boundary north to what is now Mill Street, in order to give Maynard a claim south of theirs.

3rd of April, 1852, Bell, Boren's family and Maynard moved on to the claim before the return of Boren and D. T. Denny, leaving A. A. Denny and family sick at Alki, until a house could be prepared for them on the claim.

In October, 1852, H. L. Yesler arrived from Portland, and the land claims were again readjusted to enable him to hold a claim including the site he had selected for a steam saw mill, which was the first steam mill built on the Sound.

In December, 1852, A. A. Denny and D. T. Denny discovered and explored Salmon Bay, which was previously unknown to the white settlers.

23rd of May, 1853, the first plat of Seattle was filed for record by C. D. Boren and A. A. Denny, and subsequently, on the same day, the plat of another portion was filed by D. S. Maynard.

In the winter of 1852-53 J. J. Felt arrived, and after somewhat extensive exploration located at Appletree Cove and built a mill, which he removed to Port Madison early in 1854.

85

Arthur Armstrong Denny

In the spring of 1853 Capt. William Renton came to Alki, and during the summer built a mill which he, early in 1854, removed to Port Orchard.

In April, 1853 Thomas Mercer and Dexter Horton arrived, and Mercer settled on the claim where he still lives.

Jan. 1st, 1880.

Henry, lean, Abbelt
W. N. Bell
H. L. Yesler
David T. Denny.
C. D. Boren
A. A. Denny

"Behold! Where moaned the trees . . . . .
A spreading city lies."

Plate XXXV.   —SEATTLE.

LEE TERRY.

Died in 1889.

Plate X.

"DUKE OF YORK."

Plate XI.

H S Yesler's Residence taken in 1860

(Mr. Yesler's hand writing.) Northeast corner First Avenue and James Street. The house back of Yesler's was Hillory Butler's. The Next, D. H. A. Smith's. The one opposite was S. D. Libby's. The flume is Seattle's first water works. Water flowed from a spring near what is now Fourth Avenue and James Street.

Plate XXVI.

MR. AND MRS. (Mary J. Russell) CHAS. C. TERRY
And Daughter Bess.

Plate XIII.

BISHOP MODESTE DEMERS,

Plate XV.   Who held the first religious service in Seattle.

REV. DAVID E. BLAINE AND FAMILY IN 1856.

Plate XVIII.

MRS. URSULA WYCKOFF (formerly McConaha) AND FAMILY.
The girl on the right of the group is Eugenie McConaha, the first white
child born in Seattle, Sept. 13, 1852. She died March 21, 1899.

Plate XVI.

DAVID E. BLAINE.

The First Protestant Minister stationed in Seattle. Born March 5,
1824; died November 26, 1900; Mrs. Blaine died March 9, 1908.

Plate XIX.

WILLIAM N. BELL.

Plate XIV. Died 1889. So far as known there is no picture of
Mrs. Bell.

CAPT. GUERT GANSEVOORT.
Who commanded the "Decatur" during the Indian attack on Seattle.
From a miniature painted on ivory when he was 20.

Plate XXV-a.

C. C. TERRY'S HOME.
Finest House in Seattle in the 60's. Corner Third Avenue and
James Street.

Plate XXVII.

Plate XXX.   CARSON D. BOREN.

Plate XXIX.   MRS. A. A. DENNY.

Seattle Waterfront in 1874. First Coal Bunkers, on the right, in the early 60's.

Plate XXVIII.

Index

COLOPHON

The Arthur Denny *Pioneer Days on Puget Sound*, a classic Washington state historical title, was printed in the workshop of Glen Adams, which is located in the quiet country village of Fairfield in southern Spokane County. The book was set in type by Miss Bobi Pearson using a Compugraphic 48 photosetter. The text was set in twelve point Baskerville which was given a fifteen per cent enlargement before printing. The book was stripped by Ralph Decker who also printed the sheets using a 770CD Hamada offset press. Camera-darkroom work was by Evelyn Clausen. Indexing was by Edward J. Kowrach and Becky Decker. Some of the sheets were folded by Becky Decker, who also did some of the assembly work. The rest of the assembly work was by Carol Binder, Evelyn Clausen and Edward J. Kowrach. Letterpress printing of the title page was by Glen Adams. The portrait photos of Arthur and Mary Denny were furnished by Dr. Brewster Denny of Seattle. The title page lettering is printed in 14, 18 and 24 point Bembo and 24 point Bembo Titling, all from Yendall and Company, Risca, Monmouthshire, England. The typeset border in light pale blue is from the Stephenson, Blake foundry in Sheffield, England. The paper stock is Hammermill Homespun in a seventy pound weight. This was a fun project. We had no special difficulty with the work.

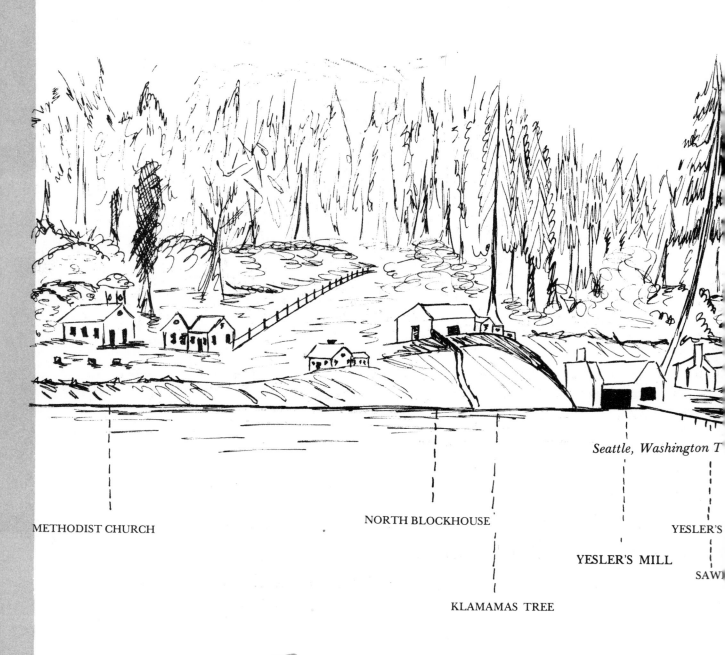

Seattle, Washington T

METHODIST CHURCH NORTH BLOCKHOUSE YESLER'S

YESLER'S MILL

SAW

KLAMAMAS TREE

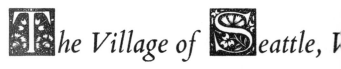

The Village of Seattle, W